the BIG GREEN

book of recycled crafts

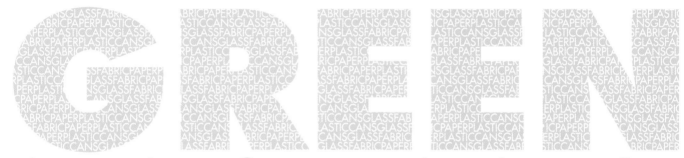

Yes, you can surround yourself with handmade beauty while helping the environment at the same time! Each project in this book uses one or more items that would ordinarily end up in a landfill. By finding ways to extend the usefulness of paper, plastic, cans, glass, clothing, and other recyclables, we've developed hundreds of green crafting ideas. Each is fun to make and even more fun to give as a gift! Whether you want to reinvent a lamp, create artwork from household discards, organize your photos, or get more mileage out of an old sweater, you'll find plenty of ideas and inspiration in these pages.

LEISURE ARTS, INC.
Little Rock, Arkansas

EDITORIAL STAFF

EDITOR-IN-CHIEF: Susan White Sullivan
CRAFT PUBLICATIONS DIRECTOR: Cheryl Johnson
SPECIAL PROJECTS DIRECTOR: Susan Frantz Wiles
SENIOR PREPRESS DIRECTOR: Mark Hawkins
ART PUBLICATIONS DIRECTOR: Rhonda Shelby
SPECIAL PROJECTS DESIGNER: Patti Uhiren
TECHNICAL WRITER: Lisa Lancaster
TECHNICAL ASSOCIATES: Frances Huddleston,
    Mary Hutcheson, and Jean Lewis
EDITORIAL WRITER: Susan McManus Johnson
SENIOR PUBLICATIONS DESIGNER: Dana Vaughn
GRAPHIC ARTIST: Janie Wright
IMAGING TECHNICIANS: Brian Hall,
    Stephanie Johnson and Mark R. Potter
PHOTOGRAPHY DIRECTOR: Katherine Atchison
CONTRIBUTING PHOTOGRAPHER: Ken West
PUBLISHING SYSTEMS ADMINISTRATOR: Becky Riddle
PUBLISHING SYSTEMS ASSISTANTS: Clint Hanson and
    John Rose

BUSINESS STAFF

VICE PRESIDENT AND CHIEF OPERATIONS OFFICER:
    Tom Siebenmorgen
DIRECTOR OF FINANCE AND ADMINISTRATION:
    Laticia Mull Dittrich
VICE PRESIDENT, SALES AND MARKETING:
    Pam Stebbins
NATIONAL ACCOUNTS DIRECTOR: Martha Adams
SALES AND SERVICES DIRECTOR: Margaret Reinold
INFORMATION TECHNOLOGY DIRECTOR:
    Hermine Linz
CONTROLLER: Francis Caple
VICE PRESIDENT, OPERATIONS: Jim Dittrich
COMPTROLLER, OPERATIONS: Rob Thieme
RETAIL CUSTOMER SERVICE MANAGER: Stan Raynor
PRINT PRODUCTION MANAGER: Fred F. Pruss

Library of Congress Catalog Number 2009925867
ISBN-13: 978-1-60140-147-2
ISBN-10: 1-60140-147-7

10 9 8 7 6 5 4 3 2 1

A PLEASANT SURGPRISE   PAGE 4

PLASTIC

TABLE

CANS

RENEW? CAN DO!   PAGE 74

PAPER

GLASS

OF *contents*

TEXTILES

THROWAWAYS

A PLEASANT *surprise*

If your recycling center can't accept all grades of plastic, check out these ideas to repurpose CD cases, plastic bags, bottles, and dryer vent hoses into decorative and useful gifts and décor. You'll be pleased to see how pretty and practical old plastic can be!

Want something useful to do with all those plastic shopping bags that pile up? Try this handy tote! First, you cut up and iron layers of bags into a sturdy, fused "fabric." Then you cut the tote front, back, and side pieces and sew them together with easy external seams and zigzag stitching. What a simple way to help save the Earth—you'll get raves from all your recycling friends!

Recycled items: plastic shopping bags (We used Target® and Old Navy™ bags because they're made of heavier plastic.)

You will also need: scissors, parchment paper, iron, and ironing surface.

Note: Use a med-high iron temperature for fusing. Experiment with some scrap bag pieces until you are comfortable with the iron temperature and ironing time needed for fusing. The fused bags should have a bumpy or wrinkled texture.

1. Lay bag out flat. Trim off bottom and handles.

2. Open bag and turn inside out.

3. Make a stack of at least 6 bags. If you want particular inked words or patterns to be a part of your design, place them right side facing up with at least 1 bag over them in the stack to preserve the ink.

4. Place enough parchment paper under and over your bags to cover them.

5. Iron one side of the parchment paper for a few seconds. Then, flip the bags and iron the other side for a few seconds. Be careful! The bags get hot.

6. Peel back a corner of parchment paper to make sure that the bags have fused completely.

7. Peel parchment paper off fused bags.

8. Fuse enough bags to cut the following pieces:

> Cut 2 – 14" x 14" squares for tote front and back.
> Cut 2 – 2" x 14" rectangles for the tote handles.
> Cut 3 – 5½" x 14" rectangles for tote sides and bottom.

Note: Use external seams and a zigzag stitch on your sewing machine.

9. Zigzag sides, front, and back together.

10. Zigzag bottom to sides, front, and back.

11. Fold in edges of handles and zigzag down the center of each handle.

12. Fold over the top edges of the tote and zigzag around the edge, inserting handles where desired on front and back.

BIRD *bungalows*

Brighten up your backyard with lively bird lodgings fashioned from colorful plastic bottles. Disposable aluminum cookie sheets or oven liners become rustic roofs, while beaded curlicues add a welcoming touch. Feathered friends will move right in!

Recycled items: large colorful plastic bottles (we used liquid laundry detergent bottles), small colorful plastic bottles with caps (we used a mustard bottle and a dishwashing liquid bottle), assorted hardware for the perch (we used a pegboard hook and a pipe bracket), bolts and nuts, assorted disposable aluminum pans, large craft needle, and plastic beads.

You will also need: utility scissors, tracing paper, repositionable spray adhesive, awl, brass paper fasteners, wire cutters, craft wire, craft crimper (for lightweight metal and paper).

1. (*Note:* If using a round bottle, cut top from bottle below handle.) For each birdhouse, refer to Fig. 1 as a guide to cut top, sides, and door and punch evenly spaced holes in large bottle.

Fig. 1

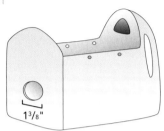

1³/₈"

2. For each topper, leaving desired length for petals, cut top section from small bottle; set bottom aside for Step 3. Cut sides and ends of petals along bottom edge of topper to create flower shape (some bottles already have a petal-shaped pattern in their design); press topper against a hard surface to bend petals outward.

3. For door flowers, trace desired flower pattern, page 143, onto tracing paper; cut out. Use repositionable spray adhesive to attach flower pattern to bottom of small bottle. Draw around pattern on bottle, then remove pattern and cut out. Aligning door and flower holes, punch through both layers as indicated on pattern; attach flower over door using paper fasteners. Use awl to punch holes for pegboard hanger or pipe bracket; use paper fasteners to attach pipe bracket. Add additional paper fasteners or bolt and nut as desired.

4. For each hanger wire, refer to Fig. 2 to attach one end of a 12" length of wire through each hole along top edge of birdhouse; use another length of wire to wrap around hanger wires to secure.

Fig. 2

5. For roof on green house, cut a 6¹/₂"w piece of aluminum pan to cover top of birdhouse and hang over edges; run piece through crimper. Cutting ¹/₂" below rim, cut a corner edge from aluminum pan the length of crimped roof piece. Overlapping one long edge of roof and flattened corner piece, use needle and wire to "sew" corner edge to front edge of roof; punch a hole in middle of roof.

6. For roof on yellow house, cut two 5¹/₂" x 14" pieces from aluminum pan; run pieces through crimper. Fold short edges of pieces together to form a tube. Gather one long edge of tube in hands to shape top of roof; pinch together.

7. Thread wires on birdhouse through hole in roof and topper, then bead. Bend three wires down. Wrap bent wires around a pencil and thread a bead onto each wire.

8. Shape end of remaining wire into a hanging loop.

Mix and match pieces from different bottles to get a variety of bright colors and interesting shapes.

These handy totes are a nifty way for kids to carry along their toys! Milk jugs and vinegar bottles make sturdy bottoms, while drawstring tops provide lots of room and easy closing. Kids will love the fun styles of these totes, and parents will appreciate their usefulness.

Recycled items: one gallon plastic container and assorted buttons.

You will also need: craft knife, small hole punch, desired fabric for bucket top, thread, two 1 yd. lengths of 1/4"w ribbon, embroidery floss, and a small safety pin to thread ribbon through casing.

For personalized bucket, you will also need: paper-backed fusible web; fabric for letters, border, and label background; 2"h alphabet stencils; black permanent fine-point marker; and thick craft glue.

1. (**Note:** We cut our round container 6" from bottom and our square container 3³/4" from bottom.) Cut container to desired height. Spacing holes approximately 1/2" apart, punch an even number of holes 1/4" below cut edge of container.

2. For fabric top, measure around cut edge; add 1/2". Cut a piece of fabric 11¹/2"h by the determined measurement. Matching right sides and using a 1/4" seam allowance, sew 11¹/2" edges together to form a tube.

3. With seam at center back and leaving 3" between top edge and buttonhole, work a 1/2" buttonhole on each side of tube for drawstring holes.

4. For casing, press top edge of tube 1/4" to wrong side. Turn pressed edge 1³/4" to wrong side again, to cover buttonholes; press. Stitch around tube 1" below top edge and along inner pressed edge. Turn fabric tube right side out.

5. Press raw edge of fabric tube 1/2" to wrong side.

6. To attach fabric to container, place bottom edge of fabric top over container to cover holes. Using floss and beginning inside container, stitch through one hole, fabric, a button, back through button, and through fabric into next hole. Repeat to attach buttons around container. (Fig. 1).

Fig. 1

7. For drawstrings, use safety pin to thread a length of ribbon into one buttonhole, through casing; and out through same buttonhole. Repeat to thread remaining ribbon through opposite buttonhole. Knot ribbon ends together on each side of fabric.

8. To make label for personalized container, use stencils to trace desired letters in reverse on paper side of fusible web. Fuse traced letters to wrong side of letter fabric; cut out. Remove paper backing and arrange letters on right side of background fabric and fuse. Cut label to desired size. Center and glue label on front of container. Cut four 1/2"w strips from border fabric to cover edges of label; glue in place.

9. Use marker to draw stitch marks around letters and along edges of label.

11

VALENTINE *sun catchers*

Pretty pastels and scallop-trimmed heart designs make our Valentine sun catchers an elegant way to adorn windows during the most romantic month of the year. Created with dimensional and acrylic paints, the window valentines are fashioned from clear plastic food containers backed with tissue paper. A string of crystal beads provides a delicate hanger for each one.

Recycled item: clear plastic food container.

You will also need: black permanent medium-point marker, black dimensional paint, white tissue paper, desired colors of acrylic paint, paintbrushes, push pin, clear thread, clear bugle beads, and craft glue.

1. For each sun catcher, cut a flat piece from plastic container. Use marker to trace desired pattern, pages 142 - 143, onto front of plastic piece.

2. Using equal parts water and glue, thin glue. Glue tissue paper to back of plastic piece; allow to dry.

3. Use dimensional paint to paint over lines on front of plastic piece; allow to dry.

4. Using equal parts water and acrylic paint, thin paint. Using dimensional paint lines as a guide, paint tissue paper; allow to dry.

5. Cut out sun catcher along outer lines of design.

6. Use push pin to make a small hole in top of sun catcher. Insert thread through hole and string beads to desired length for hanger; knot ends.

SPARKLING *sun catchers*

Your windows will sparkle and shine with these easy-to-make adornments. Great projects for creative "recycling," they're crafted from pint-size plastic berry baskets, deli plate lids, and glass paint. And with so many design possibilities, creating these colorful sun catchers is a great activity for crafters of any age!

Recycled items: pint-size plastic produce baskets and a clear plastic carry-out food container lid.

You will also need: utility scissors, black spray paint, craft glue, assorted colors of glass paint, 1/8" dia. hole punch, wire cutters, and plastic-coated craft wire.

Allow paint and glue to dry after each application.

1. For each grid, use utility scissors to cut bottom from basket. Spray paint grid black.

2. Draw around grid on lid; cut out along drawn lines.

3. Apply a thin coat of glue to back of grid; glue grid to lid piece.

4. Place glued pieces, grid side up, on a flat surface. Paint desired colors inside grid.

5. Punch a hole at each top corner of sun catcher. For hanger, thread ends of a 12" length of wire, from back to front, through holes in sun catcher; curl wire ends to secure in place.

photo frame PIZZAZZ

What to do with those empty CD cases? Transform them into sleek photo frames! It only takes a few scrapbook supplies and a little imagination.

Recycled items: CD case, scraps of poster board, and scraps of scrapbook paper or wrapping paper.

You will also need: : 5" x 7" photo, metal-look sticker with sentiment, and a craft glue stick.

1. Trim photo to 4³/₄" x 5". Cut three 4³/₄" x 5" pieces and one ⁷/₈" x 4³/₄" piece of poster board. Cut two 4³/₄" x 5" pieces and one ⁷/₈" x 4³/₄" from paper.

2. Glue each paper and photo to its corresponding size poster board.

3. Insert photo in front of CD case. Glue remaining large pieces on inside and outside of back of CD case.

4. Glue small rectangle to front of CD case and adhere sticker.

sunglass FUN

Ever wondered what to do with those old, scratched-up sunglasses? Why not use them to create mini photo frames! We simply trimmed photographs to fit in the lens spaces and then glued them in place. Personalized messages add fun to these stand-out accents.

Recycled item: sunglasses (with lenses).

You will also need: either photographs or color photocopies of photographs small enough to fit in frames of sunglasses, tracing paper, and craft glue stick, dimensional paint (optional), and beads and thread (optional).

Note: Top of glasses is bottom of frame.

1. For photograph pattern, place a small piece of tracing paper over 1 lens of sunglasses and trace shape of lens; cut out.

2. Use pattern to cut desired area from photograph.

3. Apply a thin coat of glue to back of photograph and front of lens; press photograph onto lens. Use fingertips to smooth any wrinkles or bubbles, working from center of photograph outward.

4. If desired, use dimensional paint to paint a decorative line along edges of photograph to secure photograph to lens. Paint name or occasion on remaining lens.

5. If desired, string beads onto thread to fit along top of 1 side of sunglasses frames; knot thread close to beads. Hot glue ends of thread to sides of frames to secure. Repeat for remaining side of sunglasses.

For the avid gardener, we've found the key to total organization! A five-gallon plastic bucket becomes an attractive outdoor carryall when covered with pieces of a pretty vinyl tablecloth. There are pockets all around, and a buttoned-on strap at the top provides loops for toting hand tools and other garden accessories.

Recycled items: 5-gal. plastic bucket with handle, vinyl tablecloth, twist ties, and assorted two-hole or four-hole buttons.

You will also need: clear silicone sealer, 2"w elastic, and a drill and bits.

Use silicone sealer for all gluing; allow to dry after each application.

1. For cover, measure bucket from below rim to bottom edge, then measure around bucket and add 2"; cut a piece of tablecloth the determined measurements. Fold one short edge of tablecloth piece 1" to wrong side and stitch in place. Beginning with short raw edge at back of bucket and trimming around handles, glue cover to bucket.

2. For pocket, measure around bucket and add 2"; cut a 12"w piece of tablecloth the determined measurement. Fold one short edge of tablecloth piece 1" to wrong side and stitch in place. Matching right sides and long edges, fold tablecloth piece in half; using a $1/2$" seam allowance, sew long edges together to form a tube. Turn tube right side out.

3. (**Note:** Apply glue liberally along bottom edge of bucket.) With seam of tube at bottom and beginning with raw end, wrap and glue pocket along bottom edge of bucket.

4. Measure one side of bucket between ends of handle and add 2"; cut a piece of elastic the determined measurement. Fold each end of elastic under 1"; glue ends to bucket next to handle. Repeat for remaining side of bucket.

5. Refer to Fig. 1 to mark, then drill holes in bucket through cover and elastic.

Fig. 1

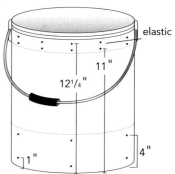

elastic

11 "

12¼ "

1 "

4 "

6. For each button, thread one twist-tie through holes in button; insert ends of twist tie through one hole in bucket and twist to secure.

7. To secure top sets of buttons inside bucket, twist ties together between top and bottom buttons.

8. To secure bottom sets of buttons inside bucket, twist ends of a third tie to ends of ties on buttons to connect top and bottom buttons.

CHARMING RING OF *vases*

Liven up your patio décor with our charming set of table vases! Each of five plastic juice bottles is trimmed with fabric and covered with a plastic piece cut from a two-liter soft drink bottle for outdoor durability. The vases are then attached to a flexible piece of plastic that secures around an umbrella pole with paper clips for easy placement and removal.

Recycled items: five 10-oz. white plastic beverage bottles, six clear plastic 2-liter beverage bottles, fabric scraps, paper clips, and raffia.

You will also need: utility scissors, spray adhesive, and household cement.

Use spray adhesive for attaching fabric; use household cement for all other gluing. Allow cement to dry after each application. Use rubber bands to hold plastic pieces in place until dry.

1. Cut tops from white bottles 1/2" below caps and discard. Cutting from center portions of clear bottles, cut one 3 1/2" x 8" piece and five 3" x 8" pieces. Cut five 3" x 8" pieces from fabric scraps.

2. For vases, overlapping ends at back and using spray adhesive, wrap and glue one fabric piece around each white bottle. Using household cement to secure ends at back, wrap and glue one 3" x 8" plastic piece over each fabric piece.

3. Tie lengths of raffia into a bow around each vase.

4. Place 3 1/2" x 8" plastic piece around umbrella pole and secure with paper clips. Space vases evenly around pole; glue to plastic piece.

BEACHCOMBER *frames*

Use and reuse a plastic container to mold plaster of paris into dozens of pretty photo frames. Just think of all the inexpensive gifts you can make!

Recycled items: large plastic container with flat bottom, cookie cutter or can to shape photograph opening, poster board, and small seashells or rope.

You will also need: craft knife, craft wire to bind ends of rope, aluminum foil, plaster of paris, desired colors of acrylic paint, paintbrush, black permanent fine-point marker, desired photograph, decorative plate stand, and thick craft glue.

1. For mold, cut around container 2" from bottom. Cover cookie cutter or can with foil; center in bottom of container.

2. If rope border is desired, cut rope to fit along inside edge of mold with ends meeting. Wrap wire around ends of rope to prevent fraying. Place rope in mold.

3. Follow manufacturer's instructions to prepare plaster. Pour plaster ³/₄" deep around cookie cutter or can. If desired, arrange shells in plaster.

4. Allow plaster to set 24 hours.

5. Remove plaster by carefully flexing mold. Remove can or cookie cutter from plaster.

6. Paint frame as desired; allow to dry. Use marker to add details.

7. Glue photograph to poster board. Centering photo in frame opening, draw around frame. Cut out ¹/₂" inside drawn line and glue to back of frame.

8. If desired, place on stand.

RECITED *bag keeper*

Our hanging keeper will organize those plastic grocery bags and keep them handy for jobs around the house. Fashioned from a plastic three-liter soda bottle and a sleeve cut from a shirt, this tidy home helper is a friend to our environment!

Recycled items: three-liter soda bottle, old shirt, and a plastic bag for hanger.

You will also need: two 6$\frac{1}{2}$" x 10" pieces of solid-colored paper, two 5$\frac{3}{4}$" x 10" pieces of striped paper, 5$\frac{3}{4}$" x 3$\frac{5}{8}$" piece of solid-colored paper, 5$\frac{1}{2}$" x 3$\frac{1}{2}$" piece of print paper, 5$\frac{1}{4}$" x 3" piece of solid-colored paper, adhesive letters, decorative-edge scissors, hole punch, and craft glue.

Allow glue to dry after each application.

1. Measure and cut 1 sleeve from shirt 14" above lower edge of cuff. Cut a 6$\frac{1}{2}$" tube from center section of soda bottle.

2. Overlapping tube 2$\frac{1}{2}$" and pleating sleeve as needed, glue raw edge of sleeve on one outside edge of plastic tube.

3. Trim each long edge of largest paper pieces with decorative-edge scissors. Overlapping short ends, glue paper pieces around plastic tube. Overlapping short ends, glue striped paper pieces on top of solid-colored pieces.

4. Trim edges of smallest paper piece with decorative-edge scissors. Layer and glue pieces on front of bag keeper. Add adhesive letters.

5. For hanger, punch a hole $\frac{3}{4}$" below top edge on opposite sides of bag keeper. Cut three 2" x 12" strips from plastic bag. Knot strips together at one end. With knot inside, thread strips through one hole. Tightly braid strips and thread ends through remaining hole; knot to secure.

BRAG *bag*

Proudly display your favorite faces with our clever "brag bag." Transform ordinary zippered clear vinyl bags into a fashionable tote by adding a vinyl strap and sewing in an extra vinyl piece to create pockets for holding photos. Braided trim and buttons make this fun accessory especially stylish.

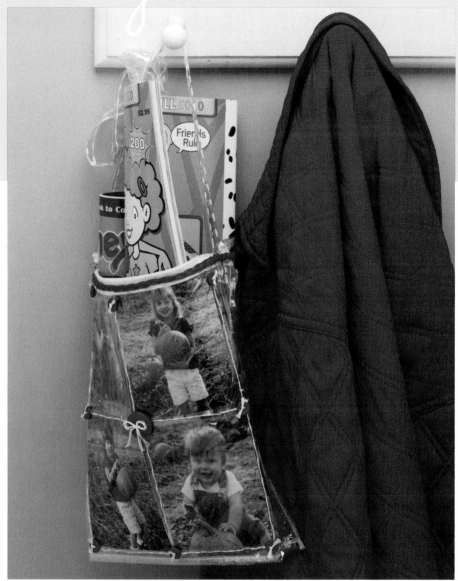

Recycled items: two clear vinyl bags with zippers, photographs, assorted buttons, and braided trim.

You will also need: embroidery floss and a low-temperature glue gun.

1. For tote, measure height and width of one bag front; subtract 1/4" from each measurement. Cut a piece of vinyl the determined measurements from remaining bag.

2. Using six strands of floss, sew bottom and sides of vinyl piece to inside front of tote; work additional stitching to form pockets to fit photographs. To insert photographs, carefully cut a slit through one layer of plastic at top of each pocket.

3. Cut a 3"w strip of vinyl the desired length for handle, piecing as necessary. Fold strip into thirds lengthwise; stitch along each long edge. Stitch one end of handle at each side of bag.

4. Use lengths of floss to sew buttons to front of tote; glue trim along top of tote.

COWBOY *lamp*

Rustle up an old pair of blue jeans and use them to create our Western lamp! A purchased lamp kit makes it easy to transform a two-liter plastic soda bottle into a fun way to light up a room. After the bottle is covered with a cut-off jeans leg, a pocket and bandanna are glued on. A lampshade decorated with pictures of the Old West rounds up this project with cowboy style!

Recycled Items: two-liter plastic bottle, sand to weight bottle, denim jeans, lampshade, and pictures from magazines.

You will also need: lamp kit for bottle base, 1 yd of ½" dia. rope, bandanna, heavy white paper, braided jute trim, spray adhesive, and a hot glue gun.

Use hot glue for all gluing unless otherwise indicated.

1. Fill bottle with sand. Follow manufacturer's instructions to attach lamp kit to bottle.

2. Remove one back pocket from jeans and cut a 16" section from bottom of one leg.

3. To cover bottle, place leg piece over bottle with hem at bottom edge of bottle. Fold top edge 2" to wrong side. Wrap rope around jeans leg 1" below top edge to gather jeans around bottle neck; glue ends of rope in place.

4. Glue side and bottom edges of pocket to front of lamp. Arrange and glue bandanna in pocket.

5. Use spray adhesive to glue pictures to heavy paper. Trim edges of paper even with pictures. Use spray adhesive to glue pictures to shade as desired.

6. Measure around top edge of shade; add ½". Cut a length of trim the determined measurement. Overlapping ends at back, glue trim along top edge of shade. Repeat to add trim to bottom edge of shade.

ARTFULLY ALFRESCO *table*

Fashioned after the expensive outdoor furniture found in specialty catalogs, our beautiful patio table provides a lot of "show" for very little dough! A plastic deli tray lid is used as a mold for the embossed concrete tabletop. After the top is attached to a wrought-iron stand, pastel paints and a cute bumblebee motif bring life to this alfresco work of art.

Recycled items: a plastic deli tray lid and a wrought-iron stand.

You will also need: ready-mix concrete; silicone adhesive; green, yellow, white, and black acrylic paint; paintbrushes; tracing paper; transfer paper; and clear acrylic sealer.

Allow silicone, paint, and sealer to dry after each application.

1. For tabletop, follow manufacturer's instructions to mix and pour 1½" of concrete into lid; allow to harden.

2. Remove hardened tabletop from lid. Use silicone to attach tabletop to stand.

3. Paint center of table green; add yellow details. Trace bee pattern, page 143, onto tracing paper. Use transfer paper to transfer design to tabletop; paint bee. Apply two coats of sealer to tabletop.

FLANNEL *flower pots*

Flowers with red, orange, and gold petals make a beautiful fall bouquet. Mums are magnificent when snuggled inside pot covers made from old flannel shirts.

Recycled items: plastic pots with saucer (we used $7^{1}/_{2}$"h x $6^{1}/_{4}$" dia. and $9^{1}/_{4}$"h x $8^{1}/_{4}$" dia. pots) and flannel shirts.

You will also need: rubber bands and a hot glue gun.

Use caution when working with glue gun.

1. For each pot, cut a circle from the back of a flannel shirt. Select a pot to fit circle by setting pot and saucer at center of circle and gathering fabric around pot at top.

2. Secure fabric at rim with a rubber band. Folding edge of fabric to wrong side, adjust gathers and hot glue fabric to pot along top edge; remove rubber band.

3. Cut button side of placket from shirt; hot glue placket around pot.

pumpkin PATCH

You don't have to make a trip to the pumpkin patch to create this charming tabletop display! Orange and green paint turn a recycled dryer vent hose and large twigs into perfect pumpkins.

Recycled items: dryer vent hose and large twigs.

For each pumpkin, you will also need: a hot glue gun, garden clippers, orange and green spray paint, 18" of medium-gauge craft wire, and 12" of 1¹/₂"w green wired ribbon.

Allow paint to dry after each application.

1. For pumpkin, with hose extended, cut a 20" to 25" length from hose. Matching open ends, form hose into a circle; glue to secure.

2. For stem, use garden clippers to cut 6" from twig.

3. Spray paint pumpkin orange. Lightly spray top of pumpkin and stem green.

4. Apply glue to one end of stem. Insert stem in opening at center of pumpkin. Curl 16" of one end of wire around a pencil; remove pencil. Wrap opposite end of wire around stem.

5. For leaves, knot ribbon around stem.

JAZZY *snowman*

When you need an extra-special delivery for holiday treats, you can count on our capricious snowman! To bring this whimsical character to life, we jazzed up a spray-painted soda bottle with craft foam cutouts.

Recycled item: two-liter plastic bottle.

You will also need: craft knife, masking tape, white and black spray paint, craft glue, clothespins, push pin, heavy-duty thread, two 3" dia. red pom-poms, tracing paper, and orange and black craft foam.

Allow paint and glue to dry after each application.

1. Mark around bottle 7" from bottom. Use craft knife to cut away top along mark.

2. For handle, cut a 1" x 13" strip from top section of bottle. Trim each end to a point.

3. Wrap handle and cover top edge of container with masking tape.

4. Spray paint outside of bottle white and handle black; allow to dry.

5. Glue one end of handle to each side of container near top edge; secure with clothespins and allow to dry. Use push pin to punch four holes through each end of handle into bottle (Fig. 1). Reinforce each end of handle by stitching an "X" through holes in handle and bottle. For ear muffs, glue a pom-pom over each end of handle.

Fig. 1

6. For face, trace nose pattern, page 143, onto tracing paper; cut out. Draw around nose pattern on orange craft foam; cut out. Rough cut two 1¼" circles for eyes and six ¾" circles for mouth from black craft foam. Glue shapes to bottle.

For a special delivery that's sure to delight a mother-to-be, give one of our sweet baby shower gift bundles. Plastic soda bottles are slit and filled with assorted items for newborns, then embellished with ribbons, flowers, and pacifiers.

Recycled item: a two-liter plastic beverage bottle for each gift bottle.

For each bottle, you will also need: small white and desired color silk flowers, white curling ribbon, 1¹⁄₂"w ribbon, pacifier with ring, assorted gift items to fill bottle, craft knife, and a hot glue gun and glue sticks.

1. (**Note:** Follow all steps for each bottle.) Use craft knife to cut a slit in back of bottle long enough to accommodate gifts. Insert gifts into bottle through slit.

2. Tie 1¹⁄₂"w ribbon into a bow around neck of bottle; trim ends.

3. Glue flowers to knot of bow.

4. Knot several lengths of curling ribbon around neck of bottle. Thread half of ribbon ends through ring on pacifier and tie ribbons into a bow; trim and curl ends.

WASTEnot

We all want to reduce the amounts of paper we purchase. But what to do with all the copy paper, packing material, bags, and boxes that still come our way? Believe it or not, these leftovers can brighten a table, help us get organized, or become a fortress for fun.

IMAGINATIVE *planter*

Let your imagination take root with this no-fuss planter. To make it, magazine pages are simply rolled into tubes and glued to a coffee can.

Recycled items: magazines and a coffee can.

You will also need: a knitting needle or dowel, desired color spray paint, a craft glue stick, and a hot glue gun.

1. Spray paint inside of can; allow to dry.

2. Cut approximately 75 pages from magazines.

3. For each tube, place a small amount of craft glue along 1 short end of magazine page. Beginning with glued end, roll page around knitting needle. Glue opposite end of page in place; remove needle.

4. Trim each tube slightly longer than height of can. Use hot glue to glue tubes around can.

WILD *wall decor*

Answer the call of the wild with exotic artwork to decorate your walls! Pick up old metal trays at a rummage sale or flea market and revive them by sponge painting and applying finger-painted "leopard spots." Add animal pictures and ribbon hangers for a unique addition to your favorite room.

Recycled items: metal tray and animal motif picture.

For each tray, you will also need: spray primer; yellow, brown, dark brown, and black acrylic paint; foam brushes; painter's masking tape; natural sponge; gold paint pen; decorative-edge craft scissors; spray adhesive; clear acrylic spray sealer; 1 yd. of 1½"w satin ribbon; and a hot glue gun.

Refer to Painting Techniques, page 157, before beginning project. Allow primer, paint, and sealer to dry after each application.

1. Clean tray and allow to dry; apply primer.

2. Paint bottom of tray black, then rim yellow.

3. Mask ends of inside bottom of tray. **Sponge Paint** center section brown; lightly sponge rim brown. Remove tape.

4. For spots, use finger to smear brown and dark brown paint on rim.

5. Use paint pen to outline brown and black sections and paint dots on black areas.

6. Use craft scissors to trim edges of motif. Apply spray adhesive to back of motif and smooth onto center of tray.

7. Apply two coats of sealer to tray.

8. Tie a bow at center of ribbon. Glue streamers to back of tray for hanger.

That drab table and chair that went unnoticed before are sure to get a second glance after being revived with paint and découpaged gift-wrap posies. Hand-painted stripes give both pieces pizzazz, so they won't be wallflowers anymore!

Recycled items: wooden folding chair with slatted back and bottom, small round wooden table, and wrapping paper.

You will also need: spray primer, two colors of acrylic paint to coordinate with wrapping paper, paintbrushes, natural sponge pieces, découpage glue, foam brushes, and clear acrylic spray sealer.

Allow primer, paint, glue, and sealer to dry after each application.

Chair
1. Apply primer, then two coats of paint to chair. Paint stripes on chair back as desired.

2. Cut a strip from paper to cover each chair slat. Follow **Découpage**, page 158, to apply strips to slats.

3. Apply two coats of sealer to chair.

Table
1. Apply primer to table. Paint table desired color. **Sponge Paint**, page 158, outer 2½" of tabletop with coordinating color of paint; paint stripes along edge of tabletop as desired.

2. Draw around tabletop on wrong side of paper; cut out 2" inside drawn line. Follow **Découpage**, page 158, to apply paper piece to tabletop. Découpage a piece of paper around spindle.

3. Apply two coats of sealer to table.

TIP

Many other types of paper products may be used to decorate your patio set. Greeting cards, wallpaper, and scrapbook paper all hold unique possibilities. You can even try fabric instead of paper.

PUZZLING *jewelry*

Mischievous shapes combine with fashionable colors and textures for a chic new look. These distinctive accessories provide a challenging use for old puzzle pieces.

Recycled items: small cardboard puzzle pieces and beads.

You will also need: gold paint pen, gold acrylic paint, paintbrushes, clear acrylic sealer, 1/8" dia. hole punch, 1/8" dia. eyelets and a setter, jewelry jump rings, clear jewelry stretch cord, jewelry wire, earring posts with attachment loops, and clear-drying jewelry glue.

1. Use the paint pen to outline the front of each puzzle piece; paint the backs and sides with acrylic paint. Apply sealer to the front and back of each piece.

2. Punch a hole in the desired number of puzzle pieces. Follow the manufacturer's instructions to attach an eyelet and a jump ring in each hole. (The earrings do not have jump rings.)

3. For bracelet, thread beads and puzzle pieces onto a length of clear stretch cord long enough to slide over your hand; knot the ends together.

TIP

Use fray preventative or glue on the ends of the cord to keep it from fraying.

4. For each earring, thread a puzzle piece onto the center of a 4" length of wire. Twist the wire tightly around itself several times to secure the puzzle piece. Thread beads onto the twisted wire, then twist one end of the wire tightly around itself to secure the beads; trim the wire end. Thread the remaining wire end through the attachment loop on the earring post; twist wire back around itself to secure in place. Glue a bead onto the post front.

WILD ABOUT *beads*

No one will ever guess that this jazzy necklace is made of items rescued from the waste basket! Create the beads using pieces cut from the rim of an aluminum baking pan and rolled-up strips from a paper bag. After painting the beads, thread them, along with ordinary wooden beads, onto a string of embroidery floss. It's the perfect necklace for casual or dressy outfits.

Recycled items: disposable aluminum baking pan, paper bag, and wooden beads.

You will also need: utility scissors; wooden skewers; black, white, cream, tan, burgundy, and brown acrylic paints; paintbrushes; craft glue; clear acrylic spray sealer; and embroidery floss.

Metal-look beads are made from the rolled, hollow rim of an aluminum pan. After cutting beads from rim, use a skewer to open up the "holes" in the beads; reshape ends as needed.

1. For metal beads, cut rim from pan. Cut 18 beads approximately $1/2$" long from rim. Rub black paint onto beads to define ridges; wipe away excess paint and allow to dry.

2. For paper beads, cut three $1^1/2$" x $9^1/4$" pieces and eight 1" x $9^1/4$" pieces from paper bag. Beginning at one end and applying a bead of glue down center of strip, roll strip tightly around skewer; glue end in place. Remove bead from skewer and allow to dry.

3. Paint animal prints on paper beads; apply two coats of sealer to beads.

4. Thread metal beads, paper beads, and wooden beads onto floss; knot ends together and trim.

Organize and protect your favorite magazines with this stylish publications holder made from a laundry detergent box. Simply cut the box to our specifications and découpage using scrunched tissue and decorative wallpaper scraps. It's so simple to make and adds a pretty touch to any décor!

Recycled items: laundry detergent box (larger in height and width than magazine to be stored in holder), white tissue paper, and decorative wallpaper scraps (we used scraps of embossed paper).

You will also need: a magazine, utility knife, white spray primer, découpage glue, foam brushes, off-white and brown acrylic paint, paintbrushes, soft cloth, and clear acrylic spray sealer.

Allow primer, glue, paint, and sealer to dry after each application.

1. For holder, draw a line around top of box 1" taller than magazine; cut top from box along drawn line. Refer to Fig. 1 to cut opening for holder.

Fig. 1

height of magazine plus 1"

width of magazine

front

2. Apply primer to entire holder.

3. Working in small sections and covering edges, apply glue to box, then press and scrunch pieces of tissue paper into glue, covering holder completely.

4. Cut sections from wallpaper to fit on front and back of holder; glue in place. Apply an additional coat of glue to outer surface of holder.

5. Paint holder off-white; apply sealer to holder.

6. For color wash, mix two parts brown paint with one part water. Working in small sections, apply wash to holder; use cloth to wipe excess from section.

7. Apply two coats of sealer to holder.

PAPER *album*

You can make a photograph album with woodsy appeal by covering an old album with brown paper grocery bags! The book is accented with a corrugated cardboard background displaying a silhouetted scene trimmed with twigs and wooden buttons for an outdoor touch.

Recycled items: photo album with binding hardware on spine, two large paper bags, corrugated cardboard, lightweight cardboard, assorted wooden buttons, and twigs.

You will also need: tracing paper, wood tone spray, spray adhesive, and a hot glue gun.

Use hot glue for all gluing unless otherwise indicated.

1. Cut bags open at seams and press with a dry iron.

2. Draw around open album once on each bag. Cut out one bag 2" outside drawn lines. Apply spray adhesive to wrong side of bag. Center open album on wrong side of bag piece. Fold corners of bag diagonally over corners of album; glue in place. Fold edges of bag over edges of album, trimming bag to fit 1/4" under binding hardware; glue in place.

3. Cut out remaining bag 1" inside drawn lines. Matching short edges, cut piece in half.

4. Apply spray adhesive to one side of each paper piece. With one edge under binding hardware, center and glue one paper piece inside front cover of album. Repeat to glue remaining piece inside back cover.

5. To decorate album cover, cut a piece from corrugated cardboard 1" smaller on all sides than front cover. Center and glue cardboard piece on front of album. Cut four twigs to fit around edges of cardboard; glue in place.

6. Trace patterns, page 144, onto tracing paper; cut out. Use patterns to cut one of each tree from lightweight cardboard and one moon and one star from corrugated cardboard. Spray cutouts with wood tone spray; allow to dry.

7. Arrange and glue cutouts and buttons on front of album. Cut pieces of twigs for tree trunks. Glue trunks under trees.

CHUNKY *candles*

When your old candles have seen better days, revive them with this resourceful "recycling" project! Using an ice cream carton as a mold, fill it with large or small chunks of old candles and pour in melted clear wax. Display on a decorative plate and accessorize with items from nature.

Recycled items: candles and an ice cream carton.

You will also need: wired candle wick, pencil, and clear candle wax.

1. Cut candles into large chunks.

2. Cut a length of candle wick 2" longer than depth of ice cream carton. Tie 1 end of wick around center of pencil. With pencil resting on sides of carton, position wick in center of carton. Fill ice cream carton with large chunks.

3. Following **Working With Wax**, page 158, melt clear wax and pour into carton; allow to harden. Tear carton away from candle.

PRETTY *place mat*

Isn't it amazing how discarded items can become decorative additions to your home? A little fabric and other supplies turn a paper grocery bag and toilet paper tube into a place mat set for your dining table.

Recycled item: paper grocery bag, toilet paper tube or wrapping paper tube, and an old button.

You will also need: fabric, embroidery floss, jute, paper-backed fusible web, and clear self-adhesive plastic (Contact® paper); optional.

1. Cut a 16½" x 11½" piece from bag; use a dry iron to press paper piece flat.

2. Follow manufacturer's instructions to fuse web to wrong side of fabric for background. Cut a 14" x 9" piece from fabric.

3. Remove paper backing from fabric. Center fabric on paper piece; fuse in place.

4. For a more durable mat, cut a piece of self-adhesive plastic slightly larger than mat; remove paper backing. Place mat right side down on adhesive plastic

and hand press in place. Trim plastic even with edges of mat. If desired, repeat to cover back of mat.

5. For napkin ring, cut a 1" section from tube. Thread floss through holes in button and tie around tube, wrapping several times; trim ends. Wrapping several times; tie jute around tube and button and knot; trim ends.

Create way-cool desk necessities for home or school using wrappers from your kids' favorite candies. Their classmates are sure to go nuts over the novelty pencils and supply keepers!

Recycled items: assorted candy wrappers, a cardboard snack canister with lid and a plastic screw-on lid from bottle for canister, and a cigar box for supply box.

You will also need: découpage glue, foam brush, soft cloths, and clear acrylic spray.

For canister, you will also need: desired colors of spray paint, a 1 1/2" dia. wooden bead for head, black permanent felt-tip pen with fine point, and a hot glue gun and glue sticks.

For each pencil, you will also need: an unsharpened pencil.

CANISTER

1. Follow **Découpage**, page 158, to découpage canister.

2. For lid, spray paint lid of canister, bead, and bottle lid for hat desired colors.

3. Use black pen to draw face on bead. Hot glue bottle lid to top of bead for hat. Hot glue bead to center of canister lid.

SUPPLY BOX

Follow **Découpage**, page 158, to découpage box.

PENCIL

Follow **Découpage**, page 158, to découpage wooden part of pencil.

"CANDIED" *camera*

Smile! You're on "candied" camera! A collage of candy wrappers and stickers, accented with bright paint, makes it easy for a young shutterbug to create a one-of-a-kind photo album cover.

Recycled items: assorted candy wrappers.

You will also need: 5" x 7" photo album, pink dimensional paint, ³/₄"h gold alphabet stickers, denatured alcohol, rubber cement, spray acrylic sealer, decorative-edge craft scissors, corrugated cardboard, black permanent medium-tip marker, and a hot glue gun.

1. Clean back of candy wrappers with alcohol. Cut wrappers into desired shapes; use rubber cement to glue wrapper shapes to album front. Spray album front with acrylic sealer; allow to dry.

2. Referring to **Painting Techniques**, page 157, use paint to outline edges of wrappers; allow to dry.

3. Use craft scissors to cut a 1¹/₄" x 4" strip of cardboard. Use stickers to spell out "PHOTOS" on one side of cardboard strip. Use marker to outline each letter. Paint edges of cardboard strip; allow to dry.

4. Glue cardboard strip onto front of photo album.

Youthful fancies will take flight when presented with this mighty play fortress! Cardboard boxes covered with paper-bag "stones" give this structure its rugged appearance. Youngsters will have hours of fun defending their stronghold against imaginary foes!

Recycled item: two large cardboard boxes for fort, additional cardboard boxes for roofs and trims, and large brown paper bags.

You will also need: craft knife, cutting mat, hot glue gun, hammer, nail, $1^{7}/_{8}$" of $^{5}/_{16}$" dia. wooden dowel, three 1" dia. wooden beads, paintbrush, brown acrylic paint, grey spray primer, and wide masking tape.

Use craft knife for all cutting unless otherwise indicated.

1. For each box, open bottom flaps and tape at side edges to make boxes taller.

2. Place boxes side by side. For doorway between boxes, cut the same size opening in facing sides of each box. Set aside cardboard cut from boxes. Matching doorway openings, glue boxes together.

3. Leaving 1 side attached, cut door in front of 1 box. Cut window flap in door.

4. Cut windows in boxes. Set aside cardboard cut from boxes.

5. For door and window frames, cut $1^{1}/_{2}$"w strips of cardboard and glue around door and windows.

6. For door handle, use hammer and nail to punch a hole in door at desired position. Thread dowel through hole. Glue one bead to each end of dowel. Glue remaining bead to back of window flap.

7. Glue top flaps of smaller box closed, if necessary. For flat roof, cut a piece of cardboard to fit box top. Glue roof to box top.

8. Open top flaps of remaining box. For front roof peak, on front of box, draw angled lines from top center of box to each side. Cut along drawn lines. Using same dimensions, repeat for back peak.

9. For peaked roof, cut a piece from cardboard to fit peaks, pieced if necessary. Fold cardboard piece in half and glue to roof peaks.

10. For shingles, cut enough 4" x 7" pieces from cardboard remnants to cover roof. Layer and glue shingles to roof. For top shingles, fold several shingles in half. Layer and glue shingles to top of roof.

11. Using a dry paintbrush and brown paint, paint window and door trim, door, top of flat roof, and shingles; allow to dry.

12. Cut each paper bag open along one fold, cutting and discarding bottom of bag.

13. For rocks, to achieve an uneven, mottled look, lightly spray unprinted sides of each bag with primer; allow to dry. Tear bags into squares of assorted sizes. Shape squares around fist. Arrange and glue rocks to fort.

TIP

The trim, door, roof, and shingles on this project are dry brushed. This technique creates a random topcoat coloration on the surface. It creates an aged look.

Do not dip brush in water. Dip paintbrush in paint; wipe most of the paint off onto a dry paper towel. Lightly rub the brush across the area to receive color. Decrease pressure on the brush as you move outward. Repeat as needed to create the desired coverage of color.

SEWING CARD *cutouts*

Sure to keep youngsters entertained, our cute sewing cards are super easy to make! Old calendar illustrations are glued to poster board and cut out. Kids can then sew lengths of colorful ribbon through holes punched in the cards.

Recycled item: wall picture calendar.

You will also need: poster board, ¼"w satin ribbon, ¼" hole punch, spring-type clothespins, spray adhesive, and fabric glue.

1. (*Note:* Follow all steps for each card.) Use spray adhesive to glue 1 calendar picture page to poster board. Cut desired shape from poster board.

TIP

Any picture can be used for the sewing cards. Simply adhere it to poster board.

2. Punch pairs of holes about 1½" apart along edges of shape.

3. Measure around edges of cutout; add 20". Cut a length of ribbon the determined measurement.

4. To stiffen each end of ribbon, apply fabric glue to about 1" of ribbon end and fold end in half lengthwise; use a clothespin to secure until glue is dry.

5. "Sew" ribbon through holes in card. Tie ends into a bow.

BIRTHDAY PARTY *favors*

What birthday party would be complete without candles! Made from bathroom tissue or wrapping paper tubes, these easy-to-make favors will be the hit of the celebration. Party guests are sure to have big smiles on their faces when they carry home your handmade container filled with goodies!

Recycled items: bathroom tissue tubes and/or wrapping paper tubes.

For each favor, you will also need: 6" x 10" piece of fabric, two 6" lengths of chenille stem, 2" triangle of orange tissue paper, 2½" triangle of yellow tissue paper, candy to fill favor, spray adhesive, and thick craft glue.

Allow glue to dry after each application. Use craft glue for all gluing unless otherwise indicated.

1. If using wrapping paper tubes, cut 4½" sections from tubes.

2. Spray outside of tubes with spray adhesive. With fabric extending at ends of tube, center and glue fabric around tube.

3. Using one length of chenille stem, gather and secure fabric at bottom of tube; stuff into tube. Fill tube with candy.

4. For wick, gather and secure fabric at top of tube with remaining chenille stem. Center orange triangle on yellow triangle. Pinch bottom edges of triangles together; glue to wick.

STATIONERY *keeper*

A favorite pen pal will love this "notable" idea for storing stationery! The perfect gift for anyone who enjoys putting pen to paper, our box has lots of room for paper and envelopes. The desktop keeper is simple to construct from a detergent box, and it will be as useful as it is decorative.

Recycled items: small detergent box and a button.

You will also need: fabric, ruler, craft knife, ribbon, spray adhesive, and a hot glue gun.

1. Refer to Fig. 1 to cut top from box.

Fig. 1

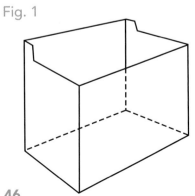

2. Follow **Covering Outside of Box**, page 158, to cover box with fabric.

3. Measure around box. Cut a length of ribbon the determined measurement. Beginning at front of box, hot glue ribbon around box. Hot glue button over ends of ribbon.

PIZZA BOX *stepping stones*

Delivered right to your door along with supper are the perfect forms for making expensive-looking stepping stones! Brick mortar is inlaid with small rocks or a handwritten message and allowed to harden in sturdy take-out pizza boxes. These outdoor accents will add a winsome touch to your garden path.

Recycled items: 4 wire coat hangers for each stone and approx. 13" take-out pizza boxes (one box may be used to make 2 to 3 stones).

You will also need: brick mortar mix (available at home centers), a large heavy-duty garbage bag, coarse sandpaper, small rocks (optional), utility knife, and 2"w packing tape.

1. Use utility knife to cut lid from box.

2. To strengthen sides of box, apply several layers of tape to top edges and sides of box.

3. Cut a square from garbage bag about 3" larger on all sides than box. Line box with plastic square.

4. To reinforce mortar, refer to Fig. 1 to place hangers in bottom of box.

Fig. 1

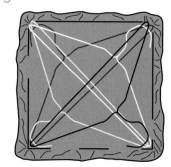

5. Follow manufacturer's instructions to mix mortar; pour mortar into box, filling box to about $1/2$" from top. Before mortar sets up, use either finger or a stick to write message in mortar or press small rocks into mortar, smoothing mortar around rocks. Allow mortar to set completely.

6. Using edges of plastic to lift stone, remove stone from box. Remove plastic from bottom of stone. If necessary, use sandpaper to smooth edges of stone.

ITTY-BITTY *gift boxes*

Even the tiniest gift seems extraordinary when you present it in a charming little box, custom made from items you already have at home. Create the itty-bitty boxes from old greeting cards, then embellish with ribbon. Lots of other pretty paper products can be used, too, such as cardstock, heavy weight stationery, or wrapping paper.

Recycled items: greeting cards.

You will also need: a hot glue gun, gifts to place in boxes, ribbon, hole punch, and grommets and a setter.

1. Reduce or enlarge desired box pattern, page 145 – 146, to fit on card; cut out. Draw around pattern on back of card. Referring to lines on pattern, cut sections on solid lines and use a ruler to fold card along dashed lines. Fold card into a box and glue sides, as necessary.

2. For square box, place gift in box, then tie a length of ribbon into a bow around box.

3. For rectangular box, use hole punch and follow manufacturer's instructions to attach grommets where indicated on pattern. Place gift in box, then thread a length of ribbon through grommets to close; tie ribbon into a bow.

Another Great Idea

Recycled items: greeting cards.

You will also need: a foam brush, craft glue, lampshade, assorted colors of rickrack, and 7" of ¼"w satin ribbon.

Allow glue to dry after each application.

1. Cut desired motifs from cards. Use foam brush to apply glue to backs of motifs. Arrange and smooth motifs on lampshade.

2. Trimming to fit, glue rickrack around top and bottom edges of lampshade. Tie ribbon into a bow. Glue bow to lampshade.

GOOD *"scents"*

Don't throw out those used dryer sheets when it makes good "scents" to turn them into pretty closet sachets like this one! A dryer sheet "bag" is simply filled with potpourri and affixed to a ribbon hanger. Clip on a "lonely" earring if desired.

Recycled item: 2 used dryer sheets and a large clip-on earring (optional).

You will also need: $6^7/_8$" x $4^1/_4$" piece each of cardstock and scrapbook or gift wrapping paper, potpourri, 1 yd of ribbon, and craft glue.

1. Iron the dryer sheets smooth. Aligning edges, place 2 dryer sheets together. Glue dryer sheets together along 1 short edge and 2 long edges.

2. Fill sachet with potpourri. Fold top over $1^1/_2$" and staple closed.

3. Glue paper to cardstock. Fold cardstock in half. Place ribbon length in crease of cardstock.

4. Glue cardstock to sachet. For hanger, tie ribbons at center. Clip earring to sachet if desired.

SANTA *wreath*

Welcome holiday guests to your home with our sensational Santa wreath! Adorned with a string of old tree lights and cutouts from greeting cards, this dapper decoration will spark Christmas cheer in folks who visit throughout the jingle bell season.

Recycled items: artificial greenery wreath, a string of Christmas lights, and greeting cards.

You will also need: a hot glue gun.

1. (**Note:** Lights should not be illuminated.) Arrange and glue lights on wreath as desired. Secure cord to back of wreath.

2. Cut desired motifs from greeting cards. Arrange and glue motifs on wreath as desired.

Another Great Idea

Recycled items: Christmas cards and colored cardstock scraps.

You will also need: matte-finish clear iron-on vinyl, colored pencils, black felt-tip pen, gold paint pen, and a pressing cloth.

1. Cut a strip from cardstock paper the desired size for bookmark. If desired, cut a slightly smaller strip from another paper and glue to bookmark. Cut piece(s) from card to fit on bookmark and glue to bookmark.

2. Use colored pencils, black pen, and paint pen to decorate bookmark and write message if desired.

3. Cut 2 vinyl strips slightly larger than bookmark. Center bookmark between strips and use pressing cloth to fuse strips together. Trim vinyl close to bookmark.

Add a fantasyland feel to your Christmas décor by transforming old ornaments into shimmering treasures! To achieve the shiny effect, glue foil candy wrappers to an ornament and embellish with acrylic jewels.

Recycled items: ornament and foil candy wrappers.

You will also need: foam brush, craft glue, assorted acrylic jewels, and gold dimensional paint.

1. Remove cap and wire from ornament.

2. Use foam brush to apply glue to wrong side of wrappers. Smooth wrappers on ornament, overlapping as necessary; allow to dry.

3. To attach each jewel, squeeze a dot of paint the same size as jewel onto ornament. Press jewel into paint; allow to dry.

4. Replace cap and wire.

Recycled items: wooden frame (we used a 16" x 20" frame), piece of fine screen larger than frame opening, uncoated paper pieces (pullout advertisement cards from magazines work great), pieces of thread (optional), and dried flowers (optional).

You will also need: a staple gun, towels, large bowls, blender, large rectangular tub (big enough for the frame to fit in easily), liquid starch, and bleached muslin pieces (at least 2" larger on all sides than the frame).

Getting Ready

1. Prepare the screen. Place the frame flat side down on screen. Pulling screen taut, staple screen to the molded side of the frame. Trim the screen even with the inner edges of the frame.

2. Prepare a surface to remove the paper from the screen. Place several towels on a flat surface, and then cover the towels with muslin.

Making the Paper

1. Tear paper into small pieces – about 1" square. Place the paper pieces in a bowl and soak in warm water for about an hour. Place 5 cups of water and a golf ball-size ball of soaked paper in blender. Blend the mixture on high for ten seconds, three or four times.

2. Pour pulp into the tub. Repeat Step 1 to fill tub to 2" from the top. If desired, add threads or dried flower pieces to the tub. Add one cup liquid starch, then stir the mixture.

Handmade paper can be expensive to purchase. But did you know you can recycle paper scraps into pretty paper for just pennies a page?

3. Holding the screen, frame side down, lower the screen into the tub down one side. Slowly pull the screen straight up out of the mixture.

4. To remove the paper from the screen, carefully place one edge of the screen on the prepared surface. Lower the screen onto the muslin, then blot the screen to remove excess water. Carefully remove screen.

Drying the Paper

1. Place the muslin and paper on an ironing surface. Place a second piece of muslin on top of the paper. Using a dry iron set on cotton, iron the stack on both sides until the paper is dry.

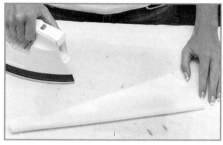

2. Peel off the top muslin piece, then lift one corner of the paper and peel it off the bottom piece.

TIP

Paper-making requires lots of pulp so you will need lots of paper pieces. A great source for paper is all that junk mail we all get. Just be sure your paper is uncoated.

STILL *shining*

It's time to see the light on recycling glass and ceramics, and we have some sparkling ideas. Besides a variety of vases, you can reuse bottles for storage and packaging gift items. Castoff windows gleam again, and orphaned dishes become a mosaic tabletop.

VALENTINE *vases*

Bouquets of fragrant blossoms will mean all the more when they're delivered in one of our valentine vases! By merely painting playful hearts, charming buds, and scribbles of sweetness, you can personalize gifts for much less than a florist shop would charge.

Recycled items: clear glass vases.

You will also need: tracing paper, removable tape, paintbrushes, and red, green, and black acrylic enamel paint.

1. Place tracing paper over patterns, page 147, and trace; cut out around patterns.

2. Tape patterns inside vases.

3. Moving patterns for desired placement of designs, paint designs on outside of vases.

UNIQUE *jars*

Mason jars are easily found in grandmother's attic, at tag sales, and antique markets. They are a staple to keep on hand, for they offer a variety of uses. Some favorites are those with windowpane embossing or a hint of blue in the glass.

SEED PACKET JAR
Recycled items: a glass jar and a seed packet.

You will also need: raffia, a button, and a hot glue gun.

1. Glue a seed packet to the front of the jar.

2. Tie raffia around the neck of the jar.

3. Tie raffia through the holes of the button; glue to the tied raffia.

FIREFLY NIGHTLIGHT
Recycled items: glass jar with lid, and assorted scrapbook stickers.

You will also need: a hammer and an awl.

1. Decorate jar with stickers.

2. Punch tiny holes in the lid.

3. Fill with insects.

FAUX *stained glass*

Searching for the perfect stained glass piece can be time-consuming — and costly. Especially when you can use a castaway window frame to create your own designer accent — inexpensively. Simply outline your pattern on the window with silver liquid leading and fill in the areas with colorful glass paint!

Recycled item: a window.

You will also need: a washable felt-tip marker, ruler, silver liquid leading, and desired colors of glass paint.

1. Use marker and ruler to draw desired design on back of glass.

2. Follow manufacturer's instructions to apply leading over lines on front of glass.

3. Follow manufacturer's instructions to paint window with glass paint.

4. Remove marker lines from back of glass.

window WITH A VIEW

Refresh your home with a lovely arrangement of botanical prints. Spray mount the flowery images onto coordinating mat boards, and then place them inside the panes of a weathered window frame. Attach a decorative drawer pull to the wood before hanging, and you're all set to enjoy your new view!

Recycled item: a window with panes and prints 1" to 2" smaller than window panes.

You will also need: mat board, craft knife and cutting mat, spray adhesive, hot glue gun, drill and bit, decorative drawer pull, and two heavy-duty sawtooth hangers.

1. Clean window frame and both sides of glass; allow to dry.

2. Cut a piece of mat board to fit each pane in window.

3. Use spray adhesive to attach a print to center of each mat.

4. Place glass and matted prints in panes; glue along edges on back to secure.

5. Attach drawer pull to center front and hangers to top back of window.

TIP

Instead of an arrangement of botanical prints, try inserting a group of coordinating scrapbook papers in the window openings.

OLD-FASHIONED *aftershaves*

Whether he's a modern man or an old-fashioned guy, a special friend will love wearing a robust after-shave you've made — and you'll love the way the nostalgic scent smells on him! Just combine bay rum with spices, citrus peel, or eucalyptus to create one of our three refreshing aromas. The presentation can be tailored to his tastes, as well. Dress up a cardboard tube with an old necktie or a little greenery, or add a hand-lettered label to give your gift personalized charm.

AFTER-SHAVES
Note: Each recipe yields 1 cup (8 oz.) of after-shave; adjust recipe as needed to fill gift bottle.

Recycled item: heat-resistant jar large enough to hold after-shave.

For each after-shave, you will need: 1 cup bay rum (available through drug stores), saucepan, cheesecloth, and the following ingredients for desired scent.

SPICY AFTER-SHAVE
1/2 teaspoon ground allspice
1/2 teaspoon ground mace
1/2 teaspoon ground cloves

CITRUS AFTER-SHAVE
2 tablespoons dried lemon peel

EUCALYPTUS AFTER-SHAVE
1/4 cup fresh or 1/8 cup dried
    eucalyptus (undyed)
1 lime peel, chopped

Pour bay rum and ingredients for desired scent into jar. Place jar in a saucepan filled half full with water; place pan over medium-high heat. Bring mixture in jar to a full boil for 1 minute. Remove from heat and allow to cool. Strain mixture through several layers of cheesecloth.

DECORATED GIFT BOTTLES
Recycled item: a decorative glass bottle with cork or lid, hot glue gun, and glue sticks.

For bottle with label and bow, you will also need: colored handmade paper, heavy ivory paper, raffia, 7" of 1"w ribbon, brown felt-tip pen with fine point, hot glue gun, and glue sticks.

For bottle with necktie wrap, you will also need: corrugated paper (available at paper supply stores), an old necktie (we found ours at a thrift store), a button, a hot glue gun, and glue sticks.

For bottle in tube with greenery, you will also need: a cardboard tube to fit around bottle, medium-weight cardboard, small grapevine wreath slightly larger than diameter of tube, artificial greenery with miniature pinecones, dried mini oak, four 3 1/2" lengths of jute twine, heavy ivory paper, and a brown felt-tip pen with fine point, hot glue gun, and glue sticks.

BOTTLE WITH LABEL AND BOW
1. For label, tear a piece of handmade paper slightly smaller than bottle front. Cut a piece of ivory paper slightly smaller on all sides than handmade paper piece.

2. Use brown pen to write "After-Shave" on ivory paper piece. Glue ivory paper piece to center of handmade paper piece. Glue label to front of bottle.

3. For bow, tie raffia lengths into a bow around neck of bottle; trim ends. Knot ribbon at center and trim ends; glue knot to raffia bow.

BOTTLE WITH NECKTIE WRAP
1. Measure bottle for desired finished height of corrugated paper. Measure around bottle; add 1/2". Cut a piece of corrugated paper the determined measurements.

2. With corrugated side of paper facing out and overlapping edges at back, glue paper around bottle.

3. For necktie trim, measure around covered area of bottle; add 1". Cut a length from narrow part of necktie the determined measurement. Press widest end of tie length 1/2" to wrong side. Beginning with unpressed end at front of bottle, glue necktie length around bottle.

4. Glue button to necktie trim.

BOTTLE IN TUBE WITH GREENERY
1. Measure bottle for desired finished height of tube. Cut a length from tube the determined measurement.

2. Draw around 1 end of tube on cardboard. Cut out circle just inside drawn circle. Glue cardboard circle just inside 1 end of tube (bottom). Center bottom end of tube on wreath; glue in place.

3. Glue a bundle of greenery and dried mini oak at top of tube. Knot lengths of twine together at center; glue knot to greenery bundle.

4. Cut tag shape from ivory paper. Use brown pen to write message on tab. Glue tag to tube near bundle of greenery.

5. Insert bottle in tube.

BEAUTY *tray*

Gussy up your bath with a pretty tray full of fancy containers to hold your beauty supplies. Bath pearls and other toiletries look exquisite in shapely bottles adorned with ribbons, lace, faux flowers, and golden charms. To give a timeworn look to a wooden tray, apply paint and crackle medium to the tray, line it with leftover or sample wallpaper, and top off the handles with frilly bows.

Recycled items: scrap of wallpaper and small glass bottles.

You will also need: wooden tray, paintbrushes, acrylic paint, crackling medium, sandpaper, craft glue, hot glue gun, items for decorating (we used ribbons, trims, sprigs of artificial flowers, charms, buttons, and acrylic jewels).

1. If necessary, refer to **Surface Preparation**, page 157, to prepare tray.

2. Follow manufacturer's instructions to apply paint and crackling medium to tray; allow to dry. Sand lightly.

3. For lining, measure length and width of inside bottom of tray; cut a piece of wallpaper the determined measurements. Use craft glue to attach wallpaper to tray.

4. Tie ribbon into bows around tray handles; glue flower springs and charms to bows.

5. To decorate bottles, use ribbon and trims to wrap bottles and tie into bows. Hot glue each bow to bottle. Glue flower sprig, charm, button, or jewel to knots of bows or to bottles as desired.

SAUCER *frame*

A perfect project for non-crafters or the very young, saucer frames also happen to look wonderful in your décor.

Recycled items: china saucer or plate.

You will also need: glue.

1. Cut photograph to fit center of saucer or plate.

2. Glue photograph to saucer or plate.

Perfect furniture for the porch or sunroom, old wrought-iron furnishings are dressed up with stunning mosaic tabletops using broken pieces of china and ceramic tiles.

Recycled item: a wrought-iron table and broken china pieces.

You will also need: ceramic tiles to coordinate with china pieces for edges of design (we used about fifteen 2¼" square tiles for the edges of our 14" x 24" tabletop), desired color tile grout (we used white), tile cutter and tile sander (if needed), ¼" plywood and saw (for tabletop base; if needed), hammer, either sandpaper or steel wool, tack cloth (if needed), old pillowcase or towel, silicone spray (if needed), and thick craft glue.

1. If covering existing tabletop, begin with Step 2. If not using existing tabletop, remove tabletop from table. To cut new tabletop base from plywood, measure width and length of top of table, measuring inside lip that holds tabletop. Subtract ⅛" from each measurement. Cut a piece of plywood the determined measurements. Lightly sand edges of plywood. Use tack cloth to remove dust.

2. (**Note:** Handle broken tile and china pieces with care. If necessary, use tile cutter to cut pieces to fit and tile sander to sand sharp edges. Keep tile and china pieces as level as possible.) For tile edges on tabletop, place tiles in pillowcase or wrap in towel; use hammer to break tiles into large pieces, retaining as many straight edges of tiles as possible for edges of table.

3. Arrange tile pieces along edges of tabletop with straight unbroken edges of tile pieces along outer edges of tabletop.

4. For design on tabletop, place china pieces in pillowcase or wrap in towel, use hammer to break china into desired size pieces. Arrange pieces on tabletop as desired. Use either tile or china pieces to fill in background around design.

5. Glue tile and china pieces to tabletop to secure. Allow to dry.

6. Follow manufacturer's instructions to apply grout between china and tile pieces on tabletop.

7. Place tabletop on table. If table will be used outdoors, spray table with silicone spray.

TIP

If you do not have access to a circular saw or table saw, many home centers will cut plywood to size on a cost-per-cut basis.

Another Great Idea
Use chipped or orphaned pieces of china to transform everyday flowerpots into fanciful patio accents by following Steps 4-6, above.

AMAZING *vases*

Just because a piece of china or glassware is one-of-a-kind, it doesn't mean it can't blossom in a new role.

Recycled item: any type of small container such as a child-size teapot, stemmed crystal goblet, sugar bowl, or porcelain teacup.

You will also need: fresh or artificial flowers.

1. Place flower in container. Display singly or in a grouping.

JAR *lantern*

When you use candle oil and your favorite items from nature, you can create an expensive-looking Jar Lantern.

Recycled item: 5¼" square x 7" h glass cracker jar with metal lid.

You will also need: artificial cranberries and key limes, plastic greenery, two 16-ounce bottles of clear lamp and candle oil, hammer and awl, 2"l x ¾" dia. bottle candle converter with fiberglass wick, and a flat-head screwdriver.

Never leave burning lantern unattended.

1. Arrange berries, limes, and greenery in jar. Fill jar with oil.

2. Use hammer and awl to punch a hole in center of lid. Adjust wick in converter so that top of wick is ⅛" above top edge of converter. Replace lid on jar, and using screwdriver to enlarge hole as needed, insert converter into hole in lid.

3. Allow wick to fully absorb oil before lighting. Trim wick if necessary to adjust flame.

Another Great Idea
Candlelight symbolically removes winter's chill, especially when the radiance spills from an old ice bucket. Cranberries add seasonal cheer and keep the candle centered.

FLORAL DELIGHT *lamp*

Bring that large empty jar out of the pantry and see it in a whole new light.

Recycled item: 4-pound honey jar.

You will also need: a jar lid lamp kit, glass etching cream, rubber gloves, clear self-adhesive plastic (Con-tact® paper), lampshade to fit lamp, heavy wrapping paper to cover lampshade, $1/4$"w satin ribbon, $1/4$" hole punch, masking tape, permanent felt-tip pen with fine point, craft knife, and craft glue.

1. Cut a 6" x 8" piece of self-adhesive plastic. Use permanent pen to trace pattern, page 148, onto center of plastic side of self-adhesive plastic.

2. Remove paper backing from plastic. With pattern centered on front of jar, place plastic on jar, smoothing bubbles and wrinkles.

3. Use craft knife to carefully cut along lines of design. Referring to pattern and leaving shaded area of design intact, remove remaining plastic from jar.

4. Cut narrow strips of masking tape to fit across sides of jar; apply to jar (we placed our strips along raised areas on sides of jar).

5. (*Note:* Follow manufacturer's instructions and wear rubber gloves when using etching cream.) Apply etching cream to front and sides of jar. Remove etching cream from jar. Remove plastic and tape from jar.

6. Follow lamp kit manufacturer's instructions to assemble lamp.

7. Refer to **Making a Pleated Lampshade**, page 159, to complete lamp.

MOTTLED BOTTLE *vases*

Fresh posies look perfectly sweet in our vibrant bottle vases. Just paint an empty jar in cheerful candy colors, then hide the threaded edge with a ring of ribbon. This winsome accent promises to enliven the patio, guestroom, or any nook or cranny.

Recycled items: assorted bottles, natural sponge, and a toothbrush.

You will also need: rubbing alcohol, white spray primer, assorted colors of acrylic paint, hot glue gun, matte clear acrylic spray sealer, and ribbon.

Refer to **Painting Techniques**, *page 157, before beginning project. Allow paint and sealer to dry after each application.*

1. Clean bottles with alcohol, then apply primer to bottles.

2. Sponge Paint each bottle with two coats of paint, then Spatter Paint each bottle with a coordinating color.

3. Apply sealer to bottles.

4. Glue end of a length of ribbon to threaded edge of bottle and wrap around bottle three times; fold end at back and glue to secure.

In the spirit of green living, here's an enlightened way to brighten your décor.

Recycled item: wine bottle.

You will also need: a bottle lamp kit, glass etching cream, rubber gloves, clear self-adhesive plastic (Con-tact® paper), self-adhesive lampshade to fit lamp, handmade paper to cover lampshade, preserved leaves, acrylic paint to coordinate with handmade paper, old toothbrush, heavy jute twine, natural raffia, spring-type clothespins, permanent felt-tip pen with fine point, craft knife, tracing paper (optional), and craft glue.

1. Measure height of straight side of bottle. Measure around bottle. Cut a piece of self-adhesive plastic the determined measurements.

2. Use permanent pen to trace leaf pattern, page 147, as desired onto plastic side of self-adhesive plastic. For pattern in reverse, trace patterns onto tracing paper and turn over before tracing onto plastic.

3. Remove paper backing from plastic. With pattern centered on front of bottle, place plastic on bottle, smoothing bubbles and wrinkles.

4. Use craft knife to carefully cut along lines of design. Referring to pattern and leaving shaded area of design intact, remove remaining plastic from bottle.

5. (**Note:** Follow manufacturer's instructions and wear rubber gloves when using etching cream.) Apply etching cream to entire bottle. Remove etching cream from bottle. Remove plastic from bottle.

6. Follow lamp kit manufacturer's instructions to assemble lamp.

7. Refer to **Spatter Painting**, page 157, to paint handmade paper.

8. Follow manufacturer's instructions to cover shade with painted handmade paper.

9. For trim at top of shade, measure around top edge of shade. Cut a length of twine the determined measurement. Beginning at shade seamline, glue twine along top edge of shade. Use clothespins to secure until glue is dry. Repeat for trim at bottom of shade. Glue preserved leaves to shade as desired.

10. Place shade on lamp.

11. Tie a length of raffia into a bow around bottle neck; trim ends.

This zesty duo is a great gourmet gift. The Pepper Sauce adds snap to vegetables and other food, and the Raspberry Vinegar adds zing to salads or favorite recipes.

Recycled items: glass bottles with lids, candle pieces for wax seal on bottle, crayon pieces to color wax, can for melting wax, cardstock for tags, and newspaper to protect work surface.

You will also need: ingredients listed for desired recipe, cotton string, funnel, pan to hold can while melting wax, permanent fine-point markers, and a hot glue gun.

1. Wash bottles and lids. Sterilize by boiling in water for five minutes; allow to dry.

2. Follow recipe to prepare and bottle vinegar.

3. Tie string around top of lid.

4. For wax seal, follow **Working With Wax**, page 158, to melt candle and crayon pieces to 2" deep.

5. Allowing wax to harden slightly between coats and holding ends of string flat against bottle, dip top of bottle in wax to completely coat lid.

6. Use markers and cardstock to make tag as desired. Glue tag to front of bottle.

Pepper Sauce

5 medium green and red hot peppers, washed, stemmed, and chopped
3 cups white vinegar

Place peppers in a 1-quart glass jar with a nonmetal lid. Bring vinegar to a simmer over medium heat. Pour vinegar over peppers and allow to cool. Cover and let stand at room temperature 1 week to let flavors blend.

Strain vinegar into gift bottles. Store in refrigerator up to 1 month.

Yield: 3 cups sauce

Raspberry Vinegar

2 packages (12 ounces each) frozen raspberries
3 cups red rice wine vinegar

Crush raspberries and combine with vinegar in a large non-aluminum saucepan. Bring to a boil over medium-high heat; boil 3 minutes. Transfer mixture to a heatproof nonmetal container. Cover and let stand at room temperature 1 week to let flavors blend.

Strain vinegar into gift bottles. Store in refrigerator up to 1 month.

Yield: 3½ cups sauce

TIP

For a heart-warming gift basket, place bottled vinegars in a straw-filled basket and tie lengths of raffia in a bow around the basket. The recipient will love it!

RENEW? *can do!*

Yes, you can keep those metal containers out of the landfills—while adding beauty to your home or that of a friend! Cheery caddies, fun gift packs, and sculptural flowers are just a few of the items you can make from discarded cans.

FENCE-RAIL *flag*

Add a touch of Americana to the backyard with this rustic flag. Paint garden stakes red and white to form the stripes and cut the gleaming stars from flattened beverage cans.

Recycled items: five aluminum beverage cans.

You will also need: white, red, and blue acrylic paint; paintbrushes; eight 36" long wooden stakes; 9¹/₂" x 16¹/₂" piece of ³/₈" plywood; saw; small nails; hammer; wood tone spray; utility scissors; and tracing paper.

Allow paint and wood tone spray to dry after each application.

1. Paint five stakes white, three stakes red, and plywood blue. Cut one white stake in half for vertical supports.

2. For flag, arrange stakes on supports; nail in place. Position plywood on flag; nail in place.

3. Lightly apply wood tone spray to flag.

4. Use utility scissors to cut through opening of each can to bottom rim; cut away and discard top and bottom.

5. Trace star pattern, page 149, onto tracing paper; cut out. Use pattern to cut fifteen stars from can pieces. Arrange stars on flag and nail in place.

When working with aluminum cans, wear gloves to protect your hands.

EN VOGUE *organizer*

Our nifty desk organizer shelf boasts a lot of animal magnetism! Juice cans and a cardboard fabric bolt are covered with trendy animal print wallpaper to fashion the "cubbies" and shelf, and a tuna can becomes a catchall container. Coordinating covered albums keep important phone numbers, addresses, and lists at your fingertips. This in-style, fun-to-create project makes getting organized a breeze!

Recycled items: five 46-oz. juice cans, 6-oz. tuna can, large scraps of coordinating wallpaper, fabric bolt, assorted buttons, small album or address book, and a brown paper bag.

You will also need: painter's masking tape, brown spray paint, craft glue, hot glue gun, decorative-edge craft scissors, and a black marker.

Use craft glue for all gluing unless otherwise indicated; allow to dry after each application.

1. Adhere tape to cans below rims. Spray paint rims and insides of cans brown and allow to dry; remove tape.

2. For each can, measure height of can between rims; measure circumference of can and add $1/2$". Cut a piece of wallpaper the determined measurements; overlapping ends, glue around can.

3. For shelf, use wallpaper to wrap bolt gift-wrap style (with overlap at bottom) using glue to secure.

4. Hot glue large cans together and to bottom of shelf. Hot glue buttons to can rims at front of organizer.

5. For each decorative cover, measure length and width of outside cover of album or address book and add 1" to length; cut a piece of wallpaper the determined measurements. Center and glue wallpaper piece to album cover, folding and gluing ends to inside of cover.

6. For album label, use craft scissors to cut a rectangle from paper bag; use marker to write on label. Glue label to front of cover.

No wallpaper scraps? Just use coordinating fabrics instead.

"CANDID" frame

Preserve a favorite image of beauty for years to come in this clever floral frame! Create the decorative flowers out of soda cans and metal bottle caps from your recycling bin.

Recycled items: five 12-oz. aluminum beverage cans, four metal bottle caps, and a wide wooden picture frame.

You will also need: utility scissors, hammer, tracing paper, transfer paper, craft foam, stylus, spray primer, brown spray paint, photo mat and cardboard (for backing) to fit in frame, paste floor wax, green acrylic paint, paintbrush, fine-grit sandpaper, tack cloth, hot glue gun, hammer, 1/2" long brass nails, clear acrylic spray sealer, removable clear tape, and a photograph to fit in mat board opening.

Allow primer, paint, and sealer to dry after each application.

1. Cut through openings in beverage cans and down to bottom rims; cut away and discard tops and bottoms of cans. Flatten can pieces. Use hammer to flatten bottle caps for flower centers.

2. Trace patterns, page 149, onto tracing paper. Place transfer paper, coated side down, between can pieces and traced pattern. Use removable tape to secure pattern to project. Use a pencil to transfer outlines of design to project. Cut out four flowers and eight leaves from can pieces (cut four leaves in reverse).

3. To emboss each flower and leaf, place shapes, printed side up, on craft foam. Pressing firmly to make indentions, use stylus to add detail lines as desired.

4. Arrange and glue flowers and leaves on frame. Nail leaves to secure; nail one flower center to each flower.

5. Apply primer, then brown spray paint to frame and mat. For distressed areas, randomly apply wax to frame and mat pieces, then paint green. Lightly sand pieces for a weathered look and wipe with tack cloth. Apply two to three coats of sealer to frame.

6. Tape photograph in opening in mat; glue mat, then cardboard backing to back of frame.

BLOOMING *luminaries*

Illuminate your patio party in style with this "blooming" garland. Simply cut aluminum cans to cover sockets on a string of miniature lights and curl narrow strips into "petals." These luminaries can be used for decorating anything from an umbrella to a backyard fence!

Recycled items: two 12-oz. aluminum beverage cans for each light cover and a string of miniature lights.

You will also need: utility scissors, awl, white spray primer, desired colors of spray paint, silicone adhesive and a paper clip.

Allow primer, paint, and adhesive to dry after each application.

1. For each light cover, draw a line around one can 3$\frac{1}{2}$" from can bottom; cut top from can along line. Use awl to make a hole at center bottom of can large enough to fit over lightbulb socket.

2. Cutting through opening in can, cut down second can to bottom rim; cut away and discard top and bottom of can. Cut a 2$\frac{3}{4}$" x 3$\frac{1}{2}$" rectangle from remaining piece.

3. For petals, make cuts $\frac{1}{4}$" apart to within $\frac{1}{2}$" from bottom of can and from one long edge of rectangle.

4. Apply primer, then two coats of paint to can pieces.

5. Wrap each petal around a pencil to curl.

6. For inner petals, overlap ends of rectangle piece $\frac{1}{2}$" and glue to secure, using paper clip to hold in place until dry. Center and glue inner petals to can bottom.

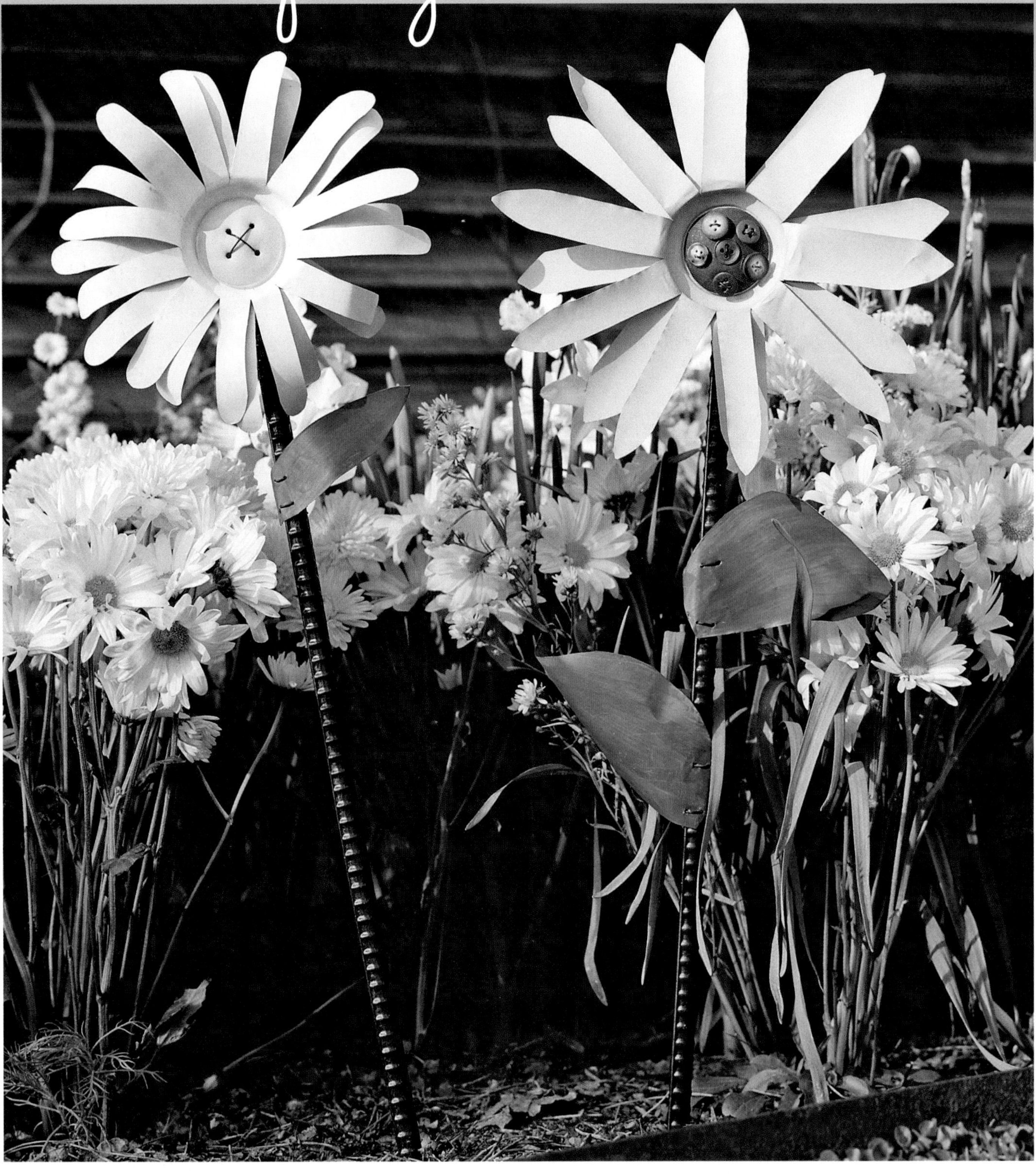

It must be spring, because flowers are popping up everywhere. Convert your soda cans and leftover buttons into whimsical blossoms.

Recycled items: 12-oz. aluminum beverage cans and assorted buttons.

You will also need: utility scissors; white spray primer; white, yellow, green, and brown acrylic paint; paintbrushes; hammer; nail; wire cutters; medium-gauge craft wire; hot glue gun; 24" rebar stake; tracing paper; and clear acrylic spray sealer.

Allow primer, paint, and sealer to dry after each application.

SUNFLOWER STAKE

1. For flower pieces, use utility scissors to cut through opening of two beverage cans; cut away and discard tops. Beginning at cut edge and cutting to within $1/2$" of bottom of can, cut down sides of each can at $5/8$" to $1 1/4$" intervals to make petals. Flatten each can with petals extending outward. Trim end of each petal to a point.

2. Apply primer to each side of each flower piece. Paint both sides of each flower piece yellow.

3. For flower center, paint inside bottom of one flower piece brown. For each "seed," use hammer and nail to punch two holes for each button along edge of flower center. Thread button onto a 4" length of wire, then wire ends through holes in flower center. Twist at back to secure.

4. Glue flower piece with "seeds" over remaining flower piece.

5. Punching through both layers, use hammer and nail to punch two holes in center of flower. Thread button onto a 6" length of wire, then wire ends through holes in flower center. Twist wire ends around rebar to secure.

6. For leaves, use utility scissors to cut through opening and down to bottom of two beverage cans; cut away and discard tops and bottoms of cans. Flatten each can piece. Apply primer to both sides of each can piece. Paint both sides of each can piece green.

7. Trace large leaf pattern, page 149, onto tracing paper; cut out. Using pattern, cut two leaves from green can pieces. Use hammer and nail to punch two sets of two holes in each leaf. Use wire to attach leaves to rebar through holes.

8. Apply two to three coats of sealer to stake.

DAISY STAKE

1. Rounding each petal, follow Step 1 of Sunflower Stake to make flower pieces.

2. Apply primer to both sides of each flower piece. Paint both sides of each flower piece white.

3. For flower center, paint inside bottom of one flower piece yellow. Glue flower piece with center over remaining flower piece. Punching through both layers, use hammer and nail to punch four holes in flower center. Forming an "X," thread ends of two 7" lengths of wire through holes in flower center. Twist wire ends around rebar to secure.

4. For leaf, use utility scissors to cut through opening and down to bottom of one beverage can; cut away and discard top and bottom of can. Flatten can piece. Apply primer to both sides of can piece. Paint both sides of can piece green.

5. Trace small leaf pattern, page 149, onto tracing paper; cut out. Using pattern, cut leaf from green can piece. Use hammer and nail to punch two sets of two holes in leaf. Use wire to attach leaf to rebar through holes.

6. Apply two to three coats of sealer to stake.

FUN *party packs*

Send your party guests home with fanciful containers filled to the rim with yummy treats! Plastic containers from ready-to-spread frosting become charming goody totes when decorated with card stock labels colorfully embellished with each guest's name. Ribbon loops make ornamental trimmings as well as convenient handles for carrying these delightful totes.

Recycled items: plastic frosting containers with lids.

For each container, you will also need: assorted colors of cardstock, decorative-edge craft scissors, black permanent fine-point marker, craft glue stick, awl, ³/₈"w ribbon, ¹/₂" dia. wooden bead, pony bead, and a hot glue gun.

Use craft glue stick for all gluing unless otherwise indicated.

1. For each treat holder, measure height, then circumference of container; cut out background from cardstock the determined measurements. Use craft scissors to cut out two ¹/₂"w strips from contrasting cardstock the circumference measurement.

2. Use marker to draw desired designs on strips.

3. Glue background around container; glue strips around background as desired.

4. For letters, enlarge alphabet patterns, page 150, 150% on photocopier and print onto cardstock; cut out letters and glue to background.

5. For handle, use awl to punch a small hole at center of lid. Thread both ends of a 10" length of ribbon through wooden bead, through hole in lid, and through pony bead; knot ribbon ends together on inside of lid. Pull handle until pony bead is snug between knot in ribbon and lid; hot glue bottom of wooden bead to lid.

"A-HEAD" OF THE *band*

Rummaging through drawers to find lost hair accessories is now a thing of the past! A large container becomes a useful headband holder when embellished with fabric, ribbon, and a button, and there's lots of room inside for barrettes.

Recycled item: 5" dia. cardboard container with a lid.

You will also need: white spray primer, assorted fabrics, spray adhesive, jumbo rickrack, hot glue gun, drawing compass, 18" of 1½"w grosgrain ribbon, tracing paper, and a button.

1. Remove lid from container. Apply primer to container; allow to dry.

2. Measure around container; add ½". Measure height of container between rims. Cut a piece from fabric the determined measurements. Apply spray adhesive to wrong side of fabric piece. Position and smooth fabric piece around container.

3. Measure around container; add ½". Cut two lengths from rickrack the determined measurement. Overlapping ends at back, glue rickrack around top and bottom of container.

4. Measure diameter of lid; multiply by 2. Using compass, draw a circle on wrong side of fabric the determined measurement. Follow Steps 1 and 2 of **Making a Fabric Yo-Yo**, page 159, to finish edge of circle. Place lid bottom side down at center of circle. Pull ends of thread to tightly gather circle over lid; knot thread ends together to secure.

5. Using ribbon, follow **Making a Ruched Flower**, page 160, to make ribbon flower. Glue ribbon flower over center gathers on lid.

6. For fabric flower, use compass to draw a 3½" circle on tracing paper; cut out. Using pattern, follow **Making a Fabric Yo-Yo** to make flower. Sew button to center of flower. Glue fabric flower over center gathers of ribbon flower.

You'll never look at those empty soda cans in the same way again! Our whimsical lamp is comprised of crushed cans threaded onto a lamp kit pipe and features a matching can-trimmed lampshade. The coordinating picture frame is created using crimped pieces of aluminum cans wrapped around a flat wooden frame. These one-of-a-kind accessories are sure to spark interesting conversation in any room!

CRIMPED CAN FRAME
Recycled items: 12-oz. aluminum beverage cans and a flat wooden picture frame.

You will also need: utility scissors, craft crimper (for paper and light-weight metal), hammer, and upholstery nails.

1. Cutting through openings in cans, cut down side of each can to bottom rim. Cut away and discard tops and bottoms of cans; flatten remaining pieces.

2. Measure thickness of frame edge; cut strips from can pieces the determined measurement. Rounding corners, cut remaining can pieces into desired shapes for front of frame. Follow manufacturer's instructions to crimp shapes and strips. Repeat to make enough pieces to cover frame, if necessary.

3. Using nails to secure, arrange and nail strips to edges, then shapes onto front of frame.

CAN LAMP BASE AND SHADE
Recycled items: brown paper (we used a grocery bag and brown kraft paper) and 12-oz. aluminum beverage cans for lamp base and shade.

You will also need: a lamp kit with base (we used a 14"h flowerpot lamp kit), découpage glue, foam brush, hammer, awl or ice pick, screwdriver, self-adhesive lampshade (we used a 7"h shade), utility scissors, craft crimper (for paper and light-weight metal), and a hot glue gun.

1. Tear pieces from brown paper. Follow **Découpage**, page 158, to cover lamp base with paper pieces; allow to dry.

2. Follow lamp kit manufacturer's instructions to assemble base and pipe of lamp.

3. Remove tabs from cans for lamp base; crush cans. Use awl to make a hole in bottom of each can through mouth in can; using screwdriver, enlarge hole to fit over lamp pipe. Leaving enough room for socket base and threading cans onto pipe, stack cans on lamp base. Complete lamp assembly.

4. Follow lampshade manufacturer's instructions to cover shade with brown paper.

5. Cutting through openings in cans for lampshade, cut down side of each can to bottom rim. Cut away and discard tops and bottoms of cans; flatten remaining pieces.

6. Rounding corners, cut can pieces into desired shapes for edges of shade. Follow manufacturer's instructions to crimp shapes. Repeat to make enough pieces to cover shade, if necessary.

7. Arrange and glue shapes along edges of shade.

A commercial can crusher is great for crushing the cans easily and uniformly.

MOSAIC KITCHEN *caddy*

Keep your cooking utensils close by with a clever kitchen caddy. Cheerful paper "tiles" transform a cardboard snack canister into this handy (and handsome) organizer.

Recycled items: cardboard snack canister and cereal boxes.

You will also need: white spray paint and craft glue.

1. Paint canister white inside and out; allow to dry.

2. Cut ³/₈" squares from the same color cardboard; leaving a small space between all pieces, glue the squares to the canister in blocks of nine.

3. Cut random shapes from another color cardboard. Leaving a small space between all pieces, glue shapes to canister to fill in remaining surface of canister.

Use marbles to weight the canister.

PATRIOTIC *table set*

Let's hear it for the red, white, and blue! Create a handy basket and silverware holder for your Fourth of July table by covering a shoe box and coffee can with commemorative fabrics. In no time, you'll have a "bang-up" way to arrange outdoor dining needs for a stars-and-stripes celebration.

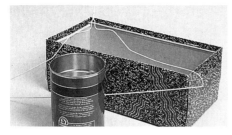

Recycled items: large shoe box, can for utensil caddy, and a white wire hanger.

You will also need: desired fabrics, desired colors of ribbon in assorted widths, poster board, hammer, nail, wire cutters, pliers, spray adhesive, and a hot glue gun.

1. Follow **Covering Outside Of Box**, page 158, to cover outside of box.

2. Follow **Covering Inside Of Box**, page 159, to cover inside of box.

3. Measure around box; add ¹/₂". Cut a length of ribbon the determined measurement. Overlapping ends at back, glue ribbon around box.

4. Tie several lengths of ribbon into a bow. Glue to front of box over ribbon.

5. To cover utensil caddy, measure around can; measure height of can. Cut a piece of poster board to fit around can. Draw around poster board piece on wrong side of desired fabric. Cut out fabric ¹/₂" outside drawn lines. Apply spray adhesive to wrong side of fabric. Center poster board piece on fabric piece.

6. On one long edge, fold corners of fabric diagonally over corners of poster board; glue. Leaving opposite long edge of fabric unturned, fold remaining edges of fabric over edges of poster board;

glue. With raw edge of fabric extending past top of can, hot glue wrong side of covered poster board around can. Glue excess fabric inside utensil caddy.

7. For handle, use hammer and nail to punch a small hole in each side of can near top edge. Cut hanger to desired length for handle. Thread one end of wire through each hole. Bend ends of wire to secure.

8. Measure around caddy; add ¹/₂". Cut a piece of ribbon determined measurement. Overlapping end at back seam, glue ribbon around caddy.

What a smart idea! You can transform ordinary food cans into charming holders for Halloween goodies. Ours use simple supplies such as spray paint, craft foam, tissue paper, fabric, curling ribbon, and chenille stems. These environmentally friendly projects are extremely economical, too.

Recycled items: small and medium cans (we used food cans and 3-oz. cat food cans), and buttons.

You will also need: green and black spray paint; yellow, dark green, and black acrylic paint; paintbrushes; orange, green, and black felt-tip pens; white and orange craft foam; $1/8$ yd fabric; orange, purple, and green tissue paper; yellow and black curling ribbon; assorted chenille stems; nail; hammer; tracing paper; transfer paper; stylus; craft knife; cutting mat; coated floral wire; wire cutters; natural raffia; glue; plastic bags or plastic wrap; and candy corn.

BASIC CAN
1. Working from inside of can, use nail and hammer to punch holes in sides of can for handles.

2. Spray paint can green or black.

3. For handle, cut a 12" length of chenille stem. Twist center of chenille stem around a pencil to curl if desired. Thread ends of chenille stem through holes in can; twist to secure.

SKULL TREAT CAN
1. Place tracing paper over pattern, page 151, and trace; cut out. Use pattern to cut one skull from white foam; cut out eyes and nose.

2. Use black pen to draw mouth and cracks on skull. Glue skull to can.

3. Tear a $3/4$" x 40" strip from fabric and tie into a bow around bottom of can.

4. Glue buttons to can. Line can with tissue paper.

PUMPKIN TREAT CAN
1. Place tracing paper over pattern, page 151, and trace; cut out. Use pattern to cut one pumpkin from craft foam; cut eyes, nose and mouth.

2. Paint pumpkin sections, stem, and leaves on foam shape.

3. For tendril, curl 5" length of floral wire around a pencil. Glue center of wire to back of pumpkin.

4. Glue foam pumpkin to can. Glue buttons to can. Line can with tissue paper.

"TRICK OR TREAT" CAN
1. Cut a piece of orange foam to fit around can.

2. Use black pen to write "TRICK OR TREAT" at center of foam piece. Glue foam piece to can.

3. Tie a length of raffia into a bow; glue to top of foam piece.

4. Glue buttons to can. Line can with tissue paper.

GREEN CAN
1. Place tracing paper over patterns, page 151, and trace; cut out. Use patterns to cut two ghosts from white foam and two small pumpkins from orange foam.

2. Use colored pens to add details to pumpkins and black pen to draw faces on pumpkins and eyes on ghosts.

3. Glue foam shapes and buttons to can.

4. Fill plastic bag or plastic wrap with candy corn; tie with lengths of curling ribbon and curl ends.

RAGS TO *riches*

They're too worn-out to wear again. And yet, throwing them away is the last thing you want to do! Turn those sweaters, linens, neckties, and jeans into useful pillows, planter covers, a blanket, or fun toy. When old wearables get a new life, we all win.

JUST "in-jean-ious"

Don't throw away those old jeans! We've found a fun and easy way to make them into a useful garden accessory. Create the unique planter by removing the legs of denim jeans and belting the waist around a clay pot. Miniature gardening tools and seed packets add a "home-grown" touch.

Recycled items: adult-size pair of denim jeans with front pockets and a belt.

You will also need: an 8½" dia. clay flowerpot with saucer, green raffia, miniature gardening tools, and seed packets.

1. Cut legs from jeans; discard legs.

2. Matching right sides, sew leg openings closed. Turn jeans right side out.

3. Place flowerpot with saucer in jeans. Thread belt through belt loops and tightly cinch belt around flowerpot to secure.

4. Tie several lengths of raffia around tool handles. Place tools and seed packets in jeans pockets.

LOCKER *pal*

What student wouldn't appreciate a way to get organized? Our inventive locker caddy is ideal for boys and girls. Four blue-jeans pockets provide spots for pencils, scissors, notes, and more!

Recycled items: two pairs of denim jeans with back pockets

You will also need: heavy-duty paper-backed fusible web, 7" x 29" piece of foam core board, hot glue gun, 72" of welting with lip, and 83" of jute twine.

1. Beginning $1^3/_4$" above back pocket, cut an 8" x 30" piece from one leg of one pair of jeans. Cut a 7" x 29" piece of web. Cutting completely through jeans, cut remaining back pockets from both pairs of jeans.

2. For background, center and fuse web to wrong side of 8" x 30" jean piece. Arrange jean piece web side down on foam core board; fuse in place. Glue edges to back of foam core board.

3. With right sides up, draw around each pocket on paper side of web; cut out and fuse to wrong side of pockets. Arrange and fuse pockets on background.

4. Trim lip of welting $^1/_8$" from stitching line. Beginning and ending at center bottom, follow **Adding Welting**, page 160, to glue welting along edges of organizer.

5. Beginning $5^1/_2$" from one end of twine and beginning and ending at center top, glue twine along edges of organizer.

6. Knot ends of twine together for hanger.

LEATHER-CLAD *lamp*

Crown a distinguished desk ensemble with this handsome creation. Castoff belts make it a cinch to revive a ragtag lamp, and tissue paper gives the shade an intriguing texture.

Recycled items: a lamp with a removable base and a center pipe tall enough to accommodate tin; tin with a lid to fit on lamp; leather remnant; assorted leather belts, including a braided belt; newspaper; lampshade to fit lamp; and a large piece of tissue paper.

You will also need: a drill and bits, craft glue, cutting mat and craft knife, removable tape, spray adhesive, and a craft glue stick.

1. Drill a hole large enough to accommodate the lamp pipe through the bottom of the tin and the center of the lid.

2. Clipping corners as necessary, glue leather remnant to the top and sides of the lid. Place the lid upside down on a cutting mat; cut an X in the leather covering the hole, then glue the leather points to the inside of the lid. Glue lid onto tin. Cut lengths from the belts to cover the sides of the tin; arrange and glue in place. Glue a belt length along the sides of the lid and the bottom edge of the tin, covering the ends of the belt lengths.

3. Remove the hardware, base, and any decorative pieces on the lamp pipe. Slide the decorated tin onto the pipe, then replace the lamp base.

4. To make a pattern of the lampshade, tape one edge of a large piece of newspaper along the seam in the lampshade. Wrap the newspaper snuggly around the shade and tape in place; cut excess paper away 1" beyond the seam in the shade. Draw along the top and bottom edges of the shade on the paper, then, leaving the paper taped to the seam on the shade, untape the outer paper and finish drawing along the shade's edges to complete the pattern. Cut excess paper away 1" outside of the drawn lines.

5. Use the pattern to cut a piece from tissue paper to cover the shade. Gently crumple the paper, then smooth it out. Apply spray adhesive to the shade, then center and smooth the paper onto the shade. Wrap the excess paper to the inside of the shade; use the glue stick to secure the paper edges in place. Glue a length of braided belt along the bottom edge of the shade. Place the shade on the lamp.

pillow TEES

No one will be able to resist cozying up to these oh-so-soft pillows! They're perfect for relaxing in front of the television or dozing on long trips in the car. A great project for using clothing outgrown by active youngsters, the pillows are made from the most comfortable thing around – T-shirts.

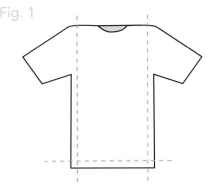

Recycled items: T-shirts

You will also need: polyester fiberfill and fabric glue.

1. For each pillow, cut hem from bottom of shirt; cut sides from shirt (Fig. 1).

Fig. 1

2. Matching right sides and raw edges, use a $1/4$" seam allowance to sew along cut edges. Turn shirt right side out.

3. Stuff pillow through neck opening. Glue neck opening closed; allow to dry.

college BOUND

Teens will enjoy "stuffing" their dirty clothes in this hanging laundry tote, especially if it's made from a T-shirt that sports their school logo. What a great gift idea for college-bound grads!

Recycled items: T-shirt and a hanger.

1. Cut hem from bottom of shirt; cut sides from shirt (Fig. 1).

Fig. 1

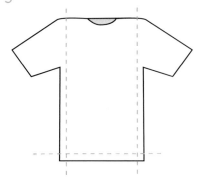

2. Matching right sides and raw edges, use a $1/4$" seam allowance and sew along cut edges of shirt. Turn shirt right side out.

3. Insert hanger in neck of shirt.

These linen accessories are perfect offerings for the woman who has everything! Covered with an antique dresser scarf, the padded hanger provides a delicate touch for an ordinary closet. The potpourri shoe sachets are made from vintage hankies and mismatched spoons. Inserting a small wind-up music box into a pillow that's easily made from another scarf adds a lovely tune to this ensemble of feminine fancies.

SHOE SACHETS

Recycled items: two silver spoons, two handkerchiefs, assorted ribbons, and silk flowers.

You will also need: batting, potpourri, and a hot glue gun.

1. For each sachet, cut a 6" circle of batting. Lay a handkerchief, wrong side up, on work surface. Center batting circle on handkerchief. Center bowl of spoon and a small amount of potpourri on batting circle.

2. Gather handkerchief at base of spoon handle. To secure handkerchief, tie several lengths of ribbon into a bow around gathers at base of handle. Glue silk flower to knot of bow.

MUSICAL PILLOW

Recycled items: dresser scarf with decorative edging and a wind-up music box.

You will also need: removable fabric marking pen, seam ripper, and polyester fiberfill.

1. Measuring from one narrow end, cut a 22" long piece from dresser scarf.

2. Determine exact center of scarf piece by folding into quarters. Make a small mark at folded point. At mark, work a buttonhole just large enough to insert handle of music box. Use seam ripper to open buttonhole.

3. Matching wrong sides and side edges of scarf piece, fold raw edge 1" past buttonhole. Fold decorative narrow edge to overlap raw edge 1/2"; pin in place. Sew side seams closed.

4. Place music box inside pillow and insert handle through buttonhole. Stuff pillow with fiberfill.

5. Use **Running Stitch**, page 160, to sew overlapped edges in place.

DECORATIVE HANGER

Recycled items: dresser scarf with decorative edging and a standard plastic clothes hanger.

You will also need: paper-backed fusible web, pressing cloth, and batting.

1. Trace around outside of hanger below hook twice onto paper side of fusible web. Draw a cutting line 1/2" outside slanted portions of hanger outlines and 1 1/2" below bottom lines; cut out.

2. For each side of hanger, position web piece on wrong side of scarf with straight edge of web 1/4" from decorative edge; fuse in place. Cut out scarf along edges of web piece; remove paper backing.

3. With pressing cloth on right side of stitched piece, fuse each stitched piece to batting. Trim batting to edges of stitched pieces.

4. Matching all edges, place right sides of stitched pieces together. Leaving bottom edges open and a 1/2" opening to insert hook of hanger at top, use a 1/4" seam allowance to sew pieces together along sides and top. Turn right side out. Insert hanger into opening.

FLANNEL SHIRT *blanket*

Flannel shirts are cuddly to wear, and they make an even cozier blanket! Our throw is a cinch to make from squares of flannel cut from worn shirts and sewn to thermal fleece.

Recycled items: flannel shirts (we used six large shirts) and 56 buttons.

You will also need: 63" x 69" piece of fleece, embroidery floss, pearl cotton (optional), and a needle.

1. Wash and dry all fabrics before beginning project.

TIP

Make a "baby" version of this blanket using fewer squares cut from recycled flannel receiving blankets.

2. Baste edges of fleece ¹/₂" to wrong side. Using pearl cotton or six strands of embroidery floss, work **Blanket Stitch**, page 160, to secure basted edges.

3. For flannel top, cut forty-two 9" squares from assorted shirts. Using a ¹/₄" seam allowance, sew seven squares into a row; repeat to make six rows. Matching right sides and seams, sew rows together along long edges.

4. Baste edges of flannel top ¹/₄" to wrong side. Center top on fleece. Using three strands of embroidery floss and **Running Stitch**, page 160, sew edges of flannel top to fleece.

5. Using three strands of floss and knotting floss on top of buttons, stitch through all layers to sew one button at each seam intersection.

NECKTIE *pillow*

Trends change from year to year, and this is especially true for clothes. Before you dump all those old ties in the garage-sale box, put them together to make a stylish pillow. Just assemble the neckties in a classic quilt pattern to fashion a new accessory for your home.

Recycled items: neckties (we used seven ties).

You will also need: seam ripper, tracing paper, 12" square of fabric for backing, 52" of ¹/₄" dia. cord, 1¹/₂" x 52" bias strip to make welting, polyester fiberfill, and thread.

Use ¹/₄" seam allowance for all sewing steps unless otherwise indicated.

1. Use seam ripper to open each tie along back seam; press open.

2. Trace patterns, pages 152 and 153, onto tracing paper. Use patterns to cut one corner piece; one piece A; and two each (one in reverse) of pieces B, C, and D from ties.

3. For pillow top, matching right sides and raw edges, sew pieces A - D together (Fig. 1).

Fig. 1

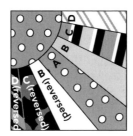

4. Press curve of corner piece ¹/₄" to wrong side. Matching curved edge of corner piece to top left corner of pillow top, topstitch along curve close to pressed edge.

5. For welting, center cord on wrong side of bias strip. Matching long edges, fold strip over cord. Using zipper foot, machine baste along length of strip close to cord. Trim seam allowance to ¹/₄".

6. Matching raw edges and using a zipper foot, start 1" from one end of welting and baste welting to right side of pillow back. Clip seam allowance as necessary. Remove 1" of basting from one end of welting and cut cord so that both ends of cord meet. Insert unopened end of welting in opened end. Fold raw edge of welting fabric ¹/₂" to wrong side; baste in place.

7. Place right sides of pillow top and back together. Stitching as close to welting as possible and leaving an opening for turning and stuffing, sew pillow top and back together. Remove basting. Clipping corners as necessary, turn pillow right side out. Stuff pillow with fiberfill; sew opening closed.

checkers ANYONE?

Checkers, anyone? Kids will be ready for a game on the go with this soft checkerboard made from time-worn blue jeans. Plastic bottle caps make great playing pieces, and the board can be rolled up for storage.

Recycled items: adult-size pair of blue denim jeans and 26 plastic bottle caps.

You will also need: straight pins, black acrylic paint, paintbrush, hot glue gun, $^3/_8$"w grosgrain ribbon, and red and black spray paint.

1. For checkerboard, cut eight $2^3/_4$" x $22^3/_4$" vertical strips and eight $2^3/_4$" x 30" horizontal strips from jeans.

2. Securing with pins and with 4" extending at each horizontal side for fringe, weave vertical and horizontal strips together.

3. Excluding fringe and stitching $^1/_4$" from outer woven edges, stitch around checkerboard. Remove pins.

4. Paint alternating squares on checkerboard black; allow to dry.

5. Trimming to fit and mitering corners as necessary, glue ribbon around checkerboard.

6. Clip fringe at $^1/_4$" to $^1/_2$" intervals to $^1/_4$" from outer edge of checkerboard.

7. For game pieces, spray paint 13 bottle caps red and 13 bottle caps black.

Can't find bottle caps? Wooden discs can be purchased at craft stores and painted for checkers.

SHIRT-POCKET *organizer*

Pocket dozens of compliments while organizing a cluttered spot with this handsome wall hanging. "Tailored" from the pockets and button cuffs of long-sleeve shirts on a fabric backing of your choosing, this organizer is a perfect fit for the home-based office.

Recycled items: nine long-sleeved shirts with pockets (with or without flaps) and button cuffs.

You will also need: utility scissors, translucent stencil plastic, two 28" squares of fabric for background and backing (may be cut from shirt backs, piecing as necessary), hot glue gun, two 1½" dia. ball-shaped wooden turnings, 30" length of 1" dia. dowel, and wood-tone spray.

1. Cut a 7½" square template from stencil plastic. With pocket centered, draw around template on shirt. Cut one square pocket piece from each shirt. Press raw edges of each square ¼" to wrong side.

2. Arrange pocket pieces on background fabric; topstitch squares along pressed edges.

3. Press top edge of background and one edge of backing piece ½" to wrong side. Matching right sides and raw edges, and leaving pressed edges open, use a ½" seam allowance to sew background and backing pieces together. Trim corners, turn right side out, and press.

4. Cut six cuffs from shirts; trim loose threads. Move buttons if necessary so that all cuffs, when buttoned, are the same diameter. Button cuffs and flatten. Placing between background and backing, space cuffs evenly along top of wall hanging. Topstitch along top edge, catching cuffs in stitching.

5. For hanger, glue turnings to ends of dowel. Apply wood-tone spray to hanger; allow to dry. Slide hanger through cuffs.

LET THE SUN *shine in*

Recycled items: scraps of assorted fabrics and rickrack, ribbons, and embroidery floss for tassels.

You will also need: ¹/₂"w paper-backed fusible web tape, ⁵/₈"w grosgrain ribbon, three large wooden beads, and three 1" dia. shank buttons.

Our valance fits a 36"w window. To adjust to fit a larger window, add additional triangles and increase or decrease amount of overlap between triangles.

1. From fabrics, cut three equilateral triangles that measure 16" on each side. For rod pocket, cut a fabric strip that measures 3" x 40".

Stitch up this colorful kitchen valance and let the sun shine in! We chose cheery orange, yellow, and green fabrics, but you may want to try other fun combinations. Beaded tassels add a touch of whimsy.

2. Press each short edge of rod pocket strip ¼" to wrong side; press ¼" to wrong side again and stitch in place. Press one long edge ½" to wrong side.

3. On two sides of each triangle, press raw edge ¼" to right side. Use web tape to fuse a length of grosgrain ribbon along each turned edge.

4. Referring to Fig. 1, overlap triangles and pin in place. Matching right sides and raw edges, use a ½" seam allowance to stitch triangles to unpressed edge of rod pocket.

Fig. 1

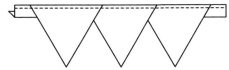

5. Referring to Fig. 2, fold pressed edge of rod pocket over raw edges and stitch in place.

Fig. 2

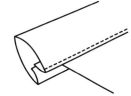

6. Fold rod pocket down over wrong side of triangles; blindstitch in place.

7. For each tassel, cut several 10" lengths of embroidery floss, rickrack and ribbon; place lengths together to form bundle. For hanger, knot a 6" length of embroidery floss around center of bundle; fold bundle in half. Thread embroidery floss and bundle through bead; glue to secure. Thread floss through button; knot and trim ends. Sew button to end of triangle.

Another Great Idea

You will need: a basket with open-weave wire sides and scraps of assorted fabrics.

1. Measure height of basket sides; multiply by three. Tear fabrics into strips 2"w by the determined measurement.

2. Loop one strip around lowest wire on basket side. With ends together, weave strip through basket side to rim; knot ends and trim to 1" long. Repeat to cover sides of basket.

COZY *sweater wrap*

Time to clean out your closet? Instead of throwing out your worn sweaters, recycle them to make a cozy afghan. We used an ensemble of natural-colored sweaters, but you can choose colorful variations to create a rainbow of snuggles.

Recycled items: 7-10 extra-large sweaters.

Match right sides and raw edges and use a ¼" seam allowance for all sewing. To prevent fraying, zigzag all raw edges.

1. Cut top portion from 5-8 sweaters, underarm to underarm (Fig. 1); discard top portions. Undo side seams to make 10-16 pieces. If necessary, trim pieces to same length. (**Note:** You may use one or more pieces from each sweater as desired.)

Fig. 1

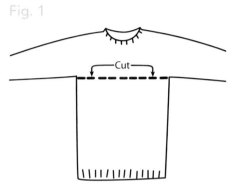

2. For each panel, sew 4 sweater pieces together along edges opposite waistband edges (Fig. 2). For afghan, matching long edges, sew panels together (Fig. 3). Trim panels to same length as needed.

Fig. 2

Fig. 3

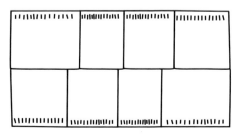

3. For each border strip, measuring 8" from edge of waistband and cutting through all layers, cut one strip from each of 2 sweaters (Fig. 4). Undo one side seam. Trimming or stretching to fit, sew borders to afghan (Fig. 5).

Fig. 4

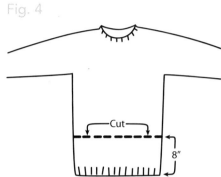

Fig. 5

BLUE JEAN *binder*

Teens are bound to love our terrific scrapbook and photo album! Castaway blue jeans are used to cover an old scrapbook or binder, and waistbands make cool button closures.

Recycled items: ring binder or scrapbook, denim jeans, lightweight cardboard, and assorted buttons.

You will also need: a hot glue gun and glue sticks.

For photo album, you will also need: fabric to cover inside of binder, 1/2 yd of "ruler" ribbon, white paint pen, and a miniature chalkboard.

For scrapbook, you will also need: fabric, a 3/4" dia. hook and loop fastener, craft knife, and mementos.

PHOTO ALBUM
1. To cover outside of binder, measure length (top to bottom) and width of open binder. Cut a piece of denim jeans 2" larger on all sides than binder, piecing as necessary.

2. Center open binder on wrong side of denim piece. Fold corners of denim diagonally over corners of binder; glue in place. Fold edges of denim over edges of binder, trimming denim to fit about ¼" under binding hardware at top and bottom; glue in place.

3. To cover inside of binder, cut two 2"w denim strips 1" shorter than length (top to bottom) of binder. Press ends ¼" to wrong side. Center and glue 1 strip along each side of binding hardware with 1 long edge tucked about ¼" under hardware.

4. Cut 2 pieces of cardboard ½" smaller on all sides than front of binder. Cut 2 fabric pieces 1" larger on all sides than 1 cardboard piece. Center 1 cardboard piece on wrong side of 1 fabric piece. Fold corners of fabric diagonally over corners of cardboard; glue in place. Fold edges of fabric over edges of cardboard; glue in place. Repeat to cover remaining cardboard piece.

5. Center and glue covered cardboard pieces inside front and back of binder.

6. (**Note:** Refer to Fig. 1 for Step 6.) Cut waistband from jeans, leaving top of each belt loop attached to waistband. For album closure, center button end of waistband along front opening edge of binder; glue to secure. Continue gluing waistband around binder to

center back; cut waistband close to center back. Remove belt loop closest to cut end of remaining end of waistband and set aside. Close binder. Fasten button into buttonhole and loosely wrap remaining waistband to back of binder. Trim waistband to meet raw end of waistband on notebook. Glue loose end of waistband to back of binder.

Fig. 1

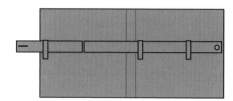

7. Glue detached belt loop over cut ends of waistband. Glue loose end of each remaining belt loop to binder.

8. Use paint pen to write "school days" on chalkboard. Arrange chalkboard and buttons on front of binder; glue in place. Tie ribbon into a bow around 1 belt loop on front of binder; trim ends.

SCRAPBOOK

1. Follow manufacturer's instructions to take scrapbook apart. Lay front and back of scrapbook flat.

2. To cover each scrapbook cover, cut a piece of fabric 1" larger on all sides than cover. Center cover right side down on wrong side of fabric piece. Fold top and bottom edges of fabric to back of cover and glue to secure. Repeat for side edges.

3. Use craft knife to make a small "X" in fabric over each existing hole in scrapbook covers.

4. Follow manufacturer's instructions to reassemble scrapbook.

5. Follow Steps 4 and 5 of Photo Album instructions to cover inside of front and back of scrapbook.

6. Cut back pockets from jeans. Arrange pockets on scrapbook; glue side and bottom edges of pockets in place.

7. For closure, cut a length from button end of waistband long enough to wrap around opening edges of scrapbook and extend 2" onto front and back covers. Glue 2" of cut end at center of opening edge on back of scrapbook. Remove 1 belt loop from remainder of waistband and glue loop to scrapbook over cut edge of waistband (Fig. 2).

Fig. 2

8. Glue 1 part of hook and loop fastener to wrong side of button end of waistband piece. Bring end to front of scrapbook. Glue remaining part of fastener to front of scrapbook to meet first part.

9. Fill pockets with mementos.

WINTRY *wrapper*

Create a clever cover for a spirited gift by putting an outdated sweater to use as a wintry bottle warmer! The snuggly wrap is quickly crafted from a sweater sleeve and scraps of paper and twine.

Recycled items: sleeve from sweater, button, and scraps of cardstock and paper.

You will also need: craft glue, hole punch, and jute twine.

1. Measure height of bottle; add 2". Measuring from finished end of sleeve, cut a piece from sleeve the determined length.

2. For bag, turn piece wrong side out. Gather cut edge and glue to secure; turn right side out. Place bottle in sleeve; turn down cuff. Sew button to cuff.

3. For tag, cut a 2³/₈" x 4³/₄" piece from cardstock and a 2¹/₈" x 4¹/₂" piece from paper. Center and glue paper piece onto cardstock. Fold tag in half. Punch a hole in folded corner of tag. Use twine to hang tag on button.

WIGGLE *worm*

This whimsical "wiggle worm" is the solution to those drafty windows and doors! Salvage the cuffs from mismatched or worn socks, sew them together, and stuff. A foam ball forms the head, and pom-poms adorn the chenille-stem antennae. Glue on button accents just for fun!

Recycled items: nine adult-size socks.

You will also need: polyester fiberfill, 4" dia. plastic foam ball, 13" of ⅜"w ribbon, tracing paper, transfer paper, white craft foam, black permanent medium-point marker, low-temperature glue gun, two bump chenille stems, two 1¼" dia. pom-poms, assorted buttons, and a ⅞" dia. bell.

1. For body, cut 4½" to 5½" long tubes from cuffs of eight socks; discard remaining portion of each sock. Sew cuff pieces together end to end to form one tube. Sew one end of tube closed. Stuff body with fiberfill.

2. For head, place plastic foam ball in toe of remaining sock. Stuff sock with fiberfill. For neck, tie ribbon into a bow around sock at bottom of head. Sew head to body.

3. Trace eyes pattern, page 151, onto tracing paper. Use transfer paper to transfer eyes to craft foam. Use marker to outline eyes. Cut out eyes. Glue eyes to head. Use marker to draw eyebrows and mouth on head.

4. For each antenna, cut a two-bump piece from one chenille stem. Work one end of antenna into head. Glue one pom-pom to remaining end of antenna.

5. Glue buttons to body as desired. Sew bell to tail.

The small buttons, pom-poms, and bell on this project could be a potential choking hazard for small children.

Denim letters are perfect for personalizing a pre-teen's room! Fashion letters from layered cardboard, using your favorite computer font as a pattern. Cover with denim or fabric scraps and decorate any way you like. What a fun way to play the "name game"!

Recycled items: corrugated cardboard, denim clothing, and craft foam scraps.

You will also need: craft glue, tracing paper, pom-poms, chenille stems, and decorative appliqués and accents.

Allow glue to dry after each application.

1. For letter patterns, enlarge computer or printed font to desired size; print letters and cut out (our K measures 12$\frac{1}{2}$" tall).

2. For each letter, draw around pattern three times on cardboard; cut out, then stack and glue cardboard letters together.

3. Cut off any double seams and remove pockets from clothing; set seams and pockets aside.

4. Clipping curves and gluing edges to back, cover one end of letter with denim piece.

5. For next denim piece, glue one edge $\frac{1}{4}$" to wrong side. Overlapping raw edge, repeat Step 4 to glue piece to letter. Continue covering with strips until letter is covered.

6. Add a pocket to one or more letters as desired. Piecing as necessary, glue seam pieces along sides of letters.

7. For each flower, trace pattern, page 151, onto tracing paper; cut out. Draw around pattern onto foam; cut out. Glue pom-pom to flower for center and chenille stem to flower for stem. Place flower in pocket.

8. Glue assorted appliqués and accents on letters as desired.

This tot-size tuffet brings to mind a favorite nursery rhyme! Chenille fabric and pom-pom fringe accent the stool, which is constructed using juice cans, cardboard, and batting. What a cute, inexpensive addition to a little one's decor!

Recycled items: chenille fabric or bedding, seven 4¹/₂" dia. x 8"h cans (we used 46-oz. juice cans).

You will also need: batting, hot glue gun, heavy-duty thread, 10" dia. cardboard circle, spray adhesive, kraft paper, and ball fringe.

1. Set aside one can for center of tuffet.

2. For each remaining can, measure height of can between rims. Measure around can. Cut a piece from batting the determined measurements. Wrap and glue batting around can.

3. Measure height of can between rims; add 4". Measure around can. Cut a piece from fabric the determined measurements. Use heavy-duty thread to baste along each long edge of fabric piece; do not trim ends. With fabric extending 2" beyond top and bottom of can, wrap and glue fabric piece around can. Pull thread ends to tightly gather fabric at top and bottom of can. Knot thread ends to secure; trim ends.

4. Arrange and glue fabric-covered cans around center can.

5. Cut a piece from fabric 1" larger than cardboard circle. Apply spray adhesive to wrong side of fabric. Clipping as necessary, smooth fabric onto cardboard. Center and glue fabric-covered cardboard onto cans for bottom of tuffet.

6. For tuffet top pattern, draw around tuffet on kraft paper; cut out. Using pattern, cut enough pieces from batting to achieve desired thickness on top of tuffet. Layer and glue batting pieces on top of tuffet. Cut one piece from fabric 1" larger on all sides than pattern. Place fabric piece on top of tuffet. Make a 1" clip in fabric between each can. Using a double strand of heavy-duty thread and turning edge of fabric to wrong side to fit along top edges, blindstitch fabric around top edges of tuffet.

7. Trimming to fit, glue a length of fringe around tuffet.

AT SECOND glance

Getting more mileage out of the things you already own is good for the environment and your budget—and there's no denying it's just plain fun! Enlighten a lampshade, convert a drawer, and pull up a new chair. You'll love them even better the second time around.

LICENSE PLATE *headboard*

Driven to collect old license plates during your flea market junkets? Then turn the fruits of your travels into a headboard that logs your various journeys. The plates are simply attached with wood screws to a piece of painted hardboard. What a great way to rev up a teenager's room!

Recycled items: (For a twin-size headboard) 21 license plates.

You will also need: a 36" x 42" piece of ¼" hardboard, two 42" long pieces of 1" x 6" lumber, black spray paint, eight 1" long wood screws, and eighty-four ⅜" long wood screws.

1. To assemble headboard, use 1" screws to attach 1" x 6" legs to back of hardboard (Fig. 1).

Fig. 1

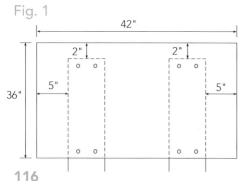

2. Paint headboard black; allow to dry.

3. Arrange license plates on headboard. Use ⅜" screws to attach plates to headboard.

"WHEELY NEAT" *nightstand*

Any automobile enthusiast will love the "engine-uity" of this bedside table fashioned from well-traveled wheel rims. Stacked in alternating sizes, the rims sport an array of colorful paints suggestive of racing flags — and they're primed for endurance! Add a glass top, and you're guaranteed a winning finish.

Recycled items: two 12" dia. and three 13" dia. wheels.

You will also need: a stiff scrub brush; spray primer; spray paint to paint wheels (we used yellow, red, blue, green, and black); silver spray paint; hot glue gun; and a 20" dia. tempered-glass tabletop.

Allow primer and paint to dry after each application.

1. Scrub wheels thoroughly with hot soapy water; rinse and allow to dry.

2. Apply primer, then two coats of desired color of paint to each wheel. Paint center of one 13" dia. wheel silver.

3. Beginning with a 13" dia. wheel and alternating sizes, stack wheels with silver wheel on top. Run a line of hot glue along top edge of nightstand; allow to harden. Place glass on nightstand.

PLAYFUL *pillars*

If you're game for a clever conversation piece, you'll love our witty creations. Simply dress up a center-burning candle with cards, checkers, puzzle pieces, marbles, even a crossword puzzle! These humorous candles are just right for setting a leisurely mood.

Recycled items: playing cards, mesh marble bag, marbles, jigsaw puzzle pieces, crossword puzzle, window screen, and checkers.

You will also need: 1/2"-long straight pins, center-burning pillar candles, hot glue gun, clear nylon thread and needle (optional), découpage glue, wire cutters, and pliers.

Caution: Use only center-burning candles. Use hot glue for all gluing unless otherwise indicated.

CARD CANDLE
1. Pinning cards in each corner, cover candle with cards turned lengthwise and face-side down.

2. Glue a second layer of cards, face-side up, on top of first layer.

MARBLE AND PUZZLE PIECE CANDLES
1. Cover outside of each candle with mesh bag, making sure bag fits snugly around candle. If necessary, cut bag to fit, then sew together with clear thread.

2. Glue marbles or jigsaw puzzle pieces to mesh. If necessary, insert pins into candle below game pieces for support.

CROSSWORD PUZZLE CANDLE
1. Cut out crossword puzzle; reduce or enlarge image to fit around candle.

2. Using découpage glue, follow manufacturer's instructions to adhere and seal puzzle around candle.

CHECKERS CANDLE
1. Cut a piece from screen to fit candle. Using pliers, bend edges of screen to inside. Wrap screen around candle; pin in place.

2. Glue checkers to screen.

CORK-POPPER'S *message board*

Pop the cork of your creativity and frame a unique arrangement of bottle stoppers for your home! This attractive bulletin board is ideal for posting reminders or telephone messages.

Recycled items: wine corks, wooden picture frame, and heavyweight corrugated cardboard.

You will also need: sandpaper, tack cloth, primer, tan and brown acrylic paint, paintbrushes, glazing medium, paper towels, hot glue gun, gimp trim, and a utility knife.

Allow paint, primer, and sealer to dry after each application.

1. If necessary, sand frame; wipe with tack cloth. Apply primer, then two coats of tan paint to frame.

2. Remove glass, if any, from frame. Mix one part brown paint with three parts glazing medium.

Brush mixture over frame; while still wet, crumple paper towel and pounce on frame randomly to create texture.

3. Trimming to fit, glue trim along opening in frame.

4. Cut a piece of cardboard to fit frame opening; glue cardboard in frame.

5. Trimming to fit, glue corks in opening of frame, covering cardboard completely.

DRAWER *ottoman*

Once a spacious dresser drawer, this unique footrest now holds thick foam padding wrapped with linen toile. Create a timeworn finish using our easy painting technique, and then add a set of turned wooden legs to heighten the classic look.

Recycled item: a wooden drawer.

You will also need: leg mounting brackets, four 6¹/₈"h wooden screw-in legs, sandpaper, tack cloth, tan and brown acrylic paint, paintbrushes, paste floor wax, wood-tone spray, clear acrylic spray sealer, eight 2" long "L" brackets, ³/₈" plywood, 4" thick foam, fabric, a staple gun, and new drawer pulls, if desired.

Allow paint, wood-tone spray, and sealer to dry after each application.

1. Remove drawer pulls from drawer. For base, use brackets to attach legs to bottom corners of drawer.

2. Sand base; wipe with tack cloth. Paint base brown, apply a thin layer of wax to base, then paint base tan. Sand base for a weathered look; wipe with tack cloth.

3. Spray base with wood-tone spray, then sealer.

4. Matching edges of brackets with top edge of base, attach two "L" brackets to each inside edge of base (Fig. 1). Replace drawer pulls on base.

Fig. 1

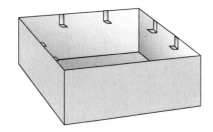

5. Measure length and width of inside base (Fig. 2). Cut a piece from plywood and foam the determined measurements.

Fig. 2

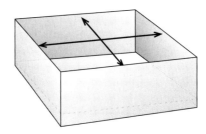

6. Draw around plywood on wrong side of fabric. Cut out 6" outside drawn lines. Place fabric, wrong side up, on a flat surface. Center foam, then plywood on fabric. Fold edges, then corners of fabric to back of plywood and staple in place. Place cushion in base.

For a more decorative ottoman, glue carved wooden appliqués to the drawer before painting. These are available at most hardware stores and home centers.

COVERED *ottoman*

An elegant yet simple project, this fabric-covered ottoman is a classy way to make something new out of something old. Drape your choice of decorative fabric over a layer of batting and staple everything to an old ottoman or footstool. Attaching deep fringe trim to the bottom edge makes a spectacular finish.

Recycled item: ottoman or footstool.

You will also need: fabric, batting, fringe, heavy-duty staple gun, screw-on wooden feet or legs (optional), and a hot glue gun.

1. If ottoman has feet or legs, remove before beginning.

2. Refer to Fig. 1 to measure from bottom edge on one side of ottoman to opposite bottom edge; add 6".

Fig. 1

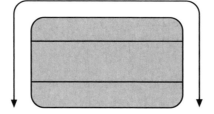

3. To cover a square ottoman, use measurement determined in Step 2 to cut three squares of batting and one square of fabric. To cover a round ottoman, follow **Cutting A Fabric Circle**, page 160, and use one-half the measurement determined in Step 2 as the string measurement to cut three batting circles and one fabric circle.

4. Center one piece of batting over top of ottoman. Pulling batting taut over ottoman and gathering excess at corners, use staple gun to staple edges of batting to underside of ottoman. Repeat for remaining batting pieces and fabric cover.

5. If desired, attach feet near bottom corners of ottoman.

6. Measure around ottoman; add 1". Cut a length of fringe determined measurement. With fringe just touching floor, glue base of fringe around ottoman.

GLOBAL *lamp*

An illuminating item for any globe-trotter, this lamp is "home-spun." Gold acrylic paint and cording add the elegant touch you need to bring a world of light into your home or office.

Recycled items: a cardboard globe and a lamp.

You will also need: a lampshade adapter, gold cord, saw, gold acrylic paint, paintbrush, and a hot glue gun.

1. For shade, cut globe in half along the equator. Paint inside of shade gold; allow to dry.

2. Trimming as necessary, glue cord around bottom of shade.

3. Follow manufacturer's instructions to attach lampshade adapter through axis hole in top of shade.

4. Place shade on lamp.

If you find it difficult to draw a straight line, but you want the effect of skilled painting, these projects are just for you. Wallpaper borders offer a multitude of designs and can be pasted to almost anything in no time!

Allow paint, glue, gel, sealer, and wallpaper to dry after each application.

Recycled item: wooden box with lid (we used a 20" dia. x 17"h box).

You will also need: items listed under **Surface Preparation**, page 157, prepasted wallpaper border, desired colors of acrylic paint, large paintbrush, small flat paintbrush, three wooden bun feet, and spray sealer.

1. Follow **Surface Preparation**, page 157, to prepare box.

2. Paint box, lid, and feet.

3. For checkerboard, lightly draw a 12" square at center of lid. Divide 12" square into sixty-four 1¹/₂" squares.

4. Paint small squares with alternating colors. Paint a ¹/₂"w border around checkerboard. Paint border around bottom of box and edge of lid as desired. Paint accents on box and lid as desired.

5. For an aged look, lightly sand painted areas; wipe clean with tack cloth. Spray box, lid, and bun feet with two or three coats of sealer.

6. Measure around box; add ¹/₂". Cut a piece of wallpaper border the determined measurement. Overlapping ends at back, follow manufacturer's instructions to apply border around box.

7. Follow manufacturer's instructions to attach feet to bottom of box.

Another Great Idea

Recycled item: wooden box (we used a 9³/₄"w x 9³/₄"d x 14"h box).

You will also need: items listed under **Surface Preparation**, page 157, prepasted wallpaper border, two colors of acrylic paint for base coat and top coat, crackle medium for acrylic paint, and a paintbrush.

1. Follow **Surface Preparation**, page 157, to prepare box.

2. Paint box with base coat. Follow crackle medium manufacturer's instructions to apply crackle medium and top coat to box.

3. For each side of box, measure width of side. Cut a piece of wallpaper border the determined measurement.

4. Follow wallpaper manufacturer's instructions to apply border pieces to box.

Turn a dated make-up travel case into a handy stationery tote in a few easy steps. Line the inside with upholstery velour, and cover the outside with soft chamois. The luxurious look and feel of these materials will encourage you to keep up your letter writing!

Recycled item: a vanity case with tray and mirror.

You will also need: velour upholstery fabric, chamois hide, ¹/₂"w gimp trim, decorative cord, spray adhesive, craft glue, and an old paintbrush.

Refer to Diagrams A and B for all measuring. Use a paintbrush to apply glue.

1. Remove fabric lining from case.

2. Measure length (A) and width (B) of inside bottom of case. Cut a piece from fabric the determined measurements. Apply spray adhesive to wrong side of fabric piece; trimming corners to fit, smooth over inside bottom of case.

3. Measure around inside edge on bottom of case (C), then measure depth of case (D); cut a strip from fabric the determined measurements. Apply spray adhesive to wrong side of strip. Matching one long edge to bottom edge of case, line inside with fabric.

4. Covering raw edges, glue gimp along top edge and cord along bottom edge of fabric. Glue a length of cord along inner edge of lid.

5. Follow Steps 2 and 3 to cover each section of tray. Covering raw edges of fabric, glue lengths of cord along top edge of tray and dividers.

6. To cover outside bottom of case, measure height (E). Measure around case (F) and add ¹/₂". Cut a piece from chamois the determined measurement. Beginning at one back hinge, applying glue to case in small sections, and trimming chamois to fit around hardware, smooth chamois piece around case; trim ends to meet. Repeat to cover top edge of case.

7. Cut a piece of chamois slightly larger than top of case. Measure distance between handles. Cut a slit the determined measurement at center of chamois piece (Fig. 1).

Fig. 1

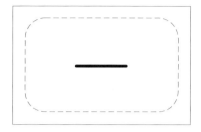

8. Insert handle through slit in chamois. Beginning at seam between handles, applying glue to top in small sections, and trimming chamois to fit around hardware, smooth chamois piece over top of case. Trim edges of chamois even with top.

DIAGRAM A

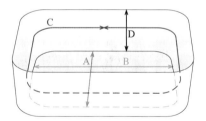

DIAGRAM B

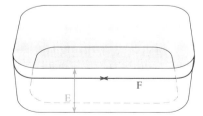

127

Ideal for dressing up the knobs of a china cabinet or armoire, these romantic tasseled adornments are made from common glass drawer pulls, beads, and an assortment of fringe, gimp, and other trims. You'll be amazed at how quickly these decorative baubles open the door to a new look for the entire room!

BULLION FRINGE TASSEL
Recycled item: glass drawer pull with hole through center.

You will also need: 3³/₄" long straight wooden clothespin, 5¹/₂" long bullion fringe, 1¹/₂" long brush fringe, ¹/₂"w decorative gimp trim, one each 18mm and 16mm faceted glass beads, 1 yd of gold 20-gauge craft wire, wire cutters, pliers, and a hot glue gun.

1. For hanger, cut two 18" lengths of wire; twist wires together. Place slit in clothespin over center of twisted wires; bring ends of wires to top of clothespin and twist once to secure.

2. Wrap and glue a length of bullion fringe around bottom of clothespin. Wrap and glue two layers of fringe just above first layer; repeat to add a third layer above second layer.

3. Wrap and glue a length of brush fringe over top of last layer of bullion fringe. Glue gimp trim around head of clothespin. Cut one strand from bullion fringe; beginning with cut end, glue strand around tassel on top of brush fringe.

4. Thread hanger wires through drawer pull, 18mm bead, then 16mm bead. Form wire into a loop; wrap wire ends around loop close to bead; trim ends.

BRUSH FRINGE TASSEL
Recycled item: glass drawer pull with hole through center.

You will also need: 5¹/₂" long brush fringe, ¹/₂"w gimp trim, two skeins #5 pearl cotton, one skein embroidery floss, 18mm faceted glass bead, and 8 mm glass bead, 5" square of cardboard, and a hot glue gun.

1. For hanger, cut four 12" lengths of pearl cotton; place lengths together and set aside. For tassel tie, cut a 6" length of pearl cotton; set aside.

2. For tassel, wrap embroidery floss and remaining pearl cotton together around cardboard. Thread hanger under threads (Fig. 1); knot hanger tightly around threads. Cut threads at bottom of cardboard. Knot tassel tie around tassel ³/₄" from hanger.

Fig. 1

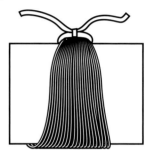

3. Beginning at tassel tie and working toward hanger, glue brush fringe around tassel. Wrap and glue gimp trim around top of fringe.

4. Thread hanger ends through drawer pull, 18mm bead, then 8mm bead. Split hanger threads in half; wrap around, then back up though 8mm bead (Fig. 2). Knot ends of hanger together.

Fig. 2

CLASSIC hamper

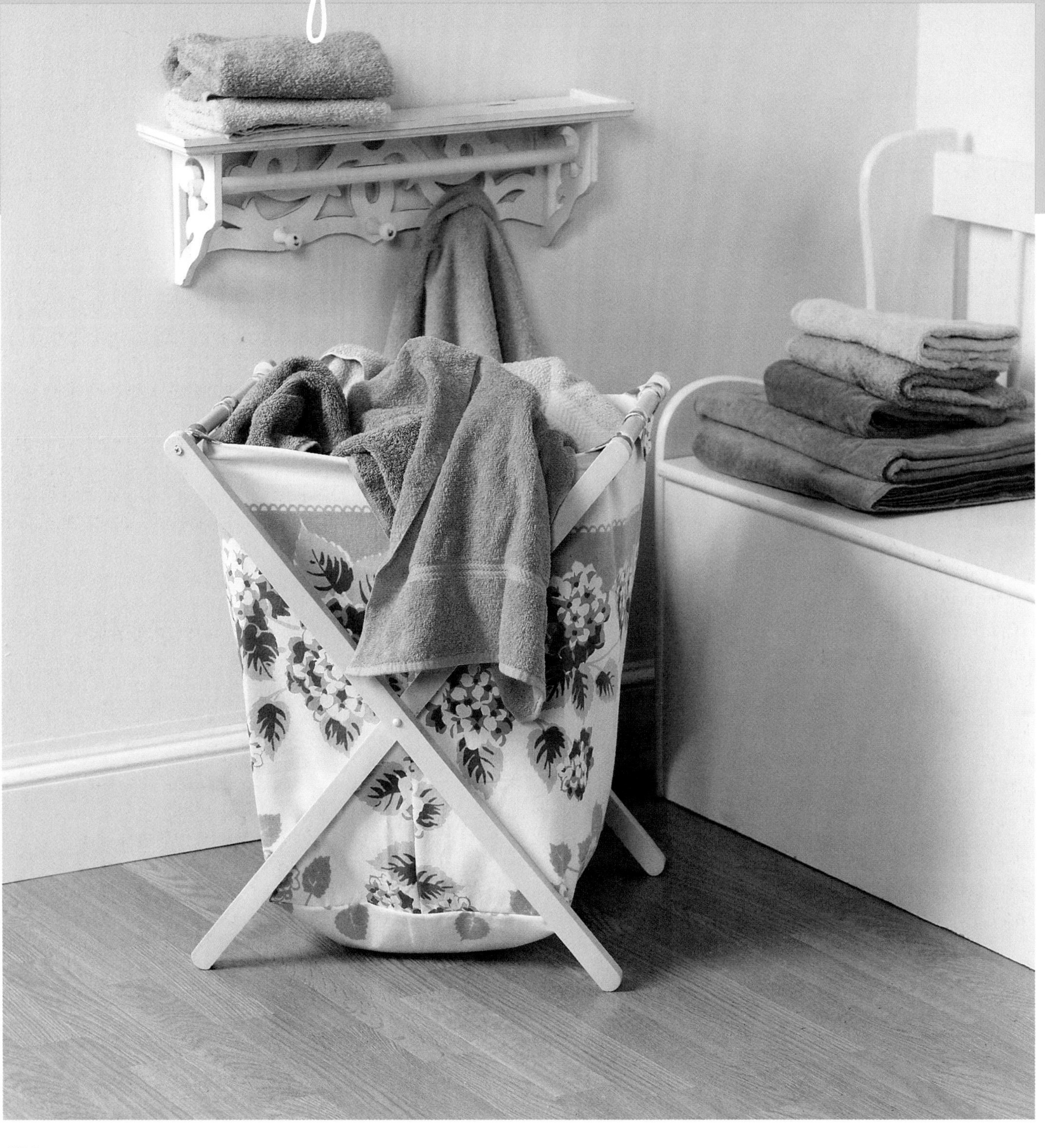

Cleverly crafted from a folding TV tray stand and a vintage tablecloth, this blooming hamper boasts classic appeal. And clean-up couldn't be easier — just unbutton the bag and add it to the wash.

Recycled items: wooden TV tray stand with tray removed, piece of string, fabric tablecloth, large fabric remnant for lining, and six buttons.

You'll also need: ³/₄" diameter wooden dowel, two wood screws, spray acrylic primer, and spray paint.

Use a ¹/₂" seam allowance for all sewing unless otherwise indicated.

1. Cut a dowel piece to fit between the top of the legs on the stand. Use screws to attach the dowel piece to the stand. Prime, then paint the stand.

2. Open the stand to the desired width, then tie a piece of string around the dowels to hold the stand's position while determining measurements.

3. Referring to Fig. 1, determine measurements for A and B; add 1" to each measurement. Cut a piece from tablecloth and one from lining fabric the determined measurements.

Fig. 1

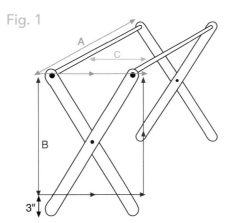

4. Matching right sides and short edges, fold the tablecloth piece in half and sew the sides together. To square the bottom, match the side seams to the bottom of the bag to form points (Fig. 2). Sew across each point (dashed lines in Fig. 2) the measurement of C from Fig. 1. Trim seam allowance to ¹/₂". Turn bag right side out.

Fig. 2

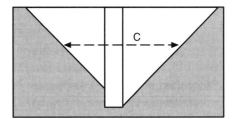

5. Leaving a 4" opening in one side seam for turning, repeat Step 4 to sew the lining together; do not turn lining right side out.

6. Cut twelve 2" x 6" strips from the tablecloth. For each tab, match the right sides of two strips together and sew the sides and one end together; turn right-side out. Make a buttonhole in the sewn end.

7. Matching side seams, fold bag to find center front and back along top edge (Fig. 3); mark. Matching right sides and raw edges, pin one tab to the bag at each mark. Evenly spacing tabs across the dowels, pin tabs to the bag and around the dowels. Adjust tabs as needed and mark placements for buttons on bag. Remove the bag from the dowels and baste the tabs in place.

Fig. 3

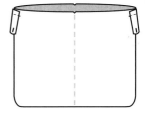

8. Matching right sides, raw edges, and side seams, place the tablecloth bag inside the lining and sew the top edges together. Turn the bag right side out through the opening in the lining, then stitch the opening closed.

9. Sew the buttons to the bag. Place the bag in the stand and button the tabs around the dowels.

CHALKBOARD *floorcloth*

With just a few coats of paint and some easy stenciling, a scrap piece of vinyl flooring becomes a cheerful floorcloth for kids. This chalkboard-look project includes a special feature — Kids can really write on it.

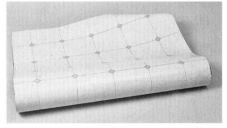

Recycled item: piece of vinyl flooring (we used a 24" x 36" piece of vinyl).

You will also need: flat black spray paint, removable tape, white acrylic paint, $3/8$"w and $5/8$"w flat-edge paintbrushes, alphabet and number stencils, desired colors of acrylic paint, sponge, and spray matte sealer.

Allow paint and sealer to dry after each application.

1. Apply two coats of black paint to the wrong side of vinyl flooring piece.

2. For inner border, place a strip of tape $4^1/2$" inside edge around all sides of flooring piece. Place a second strip of tape $1/2$" outside first strip around all sides. Use $3/8$"w paintbrush to paint evenly spaced white marks between strips of tape.

3. For outer border, place a strip of tape $5/8$" inside all edges of flooring piece. Use $5/8$"w paintbrush to paint evenly spaced white marks along outer edge.

4. Remove tape. Use stencils, sponge, and desired color paint to paint alphabet and numbers inside borders.

5. Spray entire surface with sealer.

FANCIFUL *memo board*

The glass in an old picture frame provides an ideal surface for writing notes with a dry-erase marker. Simply decorate the back of the glass as you please and spray it with white paint; then dress up the frame with whimsical stripes and swirls. The result is a fanciful memo board guaranteed to catch the eye of all passersby!

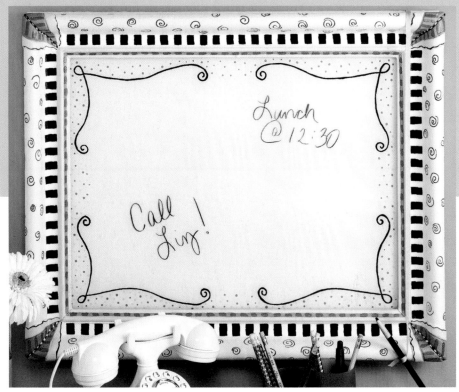

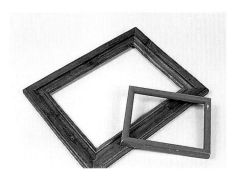

Recycled item: picture frame.

You will also need: spray primer, assorted colors of acrylic paint, paintbrushes, matte clear acrylic spray sealer, glass to fit in frame, paint pens, and matte-finish white spray paint.

Refer to **Painting Techniques**, page 157, before beginning project. Allow primer, paint, and sealer to dry after each application. Only use a grease pencil or a dry-erase pen on glass.

1. Apply primer to frame. Paint frame as desired (we painted striped borders, dots, and swirls over our basecoat colors). Apply sealer to frame.

2. Paint design on glass as desired (we used a paint pen to draw swirled lines and the end of a paintbrush handle to paint the dots). Spray painted side of glass white.

3. With unpainted side of glass facing front, mount glass in frame.

CAREFREE *thoughts*

Sometimes old things just need a perky new look to make them useful again. That was true for this lampshade. See how it shines now!

Recycled items: scraps of white trim, white cording, and white lip cording; and a lamp with shade.

You will also need: white fabric, tissue paper, clear tape, spray adhesive, fabric glue, and liquid fray preventative.

1. Follow **Covering A Flat Lampshade**, page 159, to cover shade with white fabric.

2. With lip on outside of shade, glue lip cording around top and bottom edges of shade. Glue trim onto lip.

3. Cut varying lengths of cording; apply liquid fray preventative to ends. Arrange lengths in looped patterns on shade; glue in place.

RADIANT *ribbons*

Another easy way to give an old lamp a vibrant new personality is to add scrap ribbons to its shade.

Recycled items: scraps of orange and pink ribbon and a lamp with shade.

You will also need: yellow fabric, clear tape, spray adhesive, fabric glue, and tissue paper.

1. Follow **Covering A Flat Lampshade**, page 159, to cover shade with yellow fabric.

2. Measure height of shade. Add 1" and cut ribbons this length.

3. To attach each ribbon, wrap and glue ribbon to inside of shade at top and bottom. Continue attaching ribbons until shade is covered.

4. Glue narrow pink ribbons around inside top and inside bottom of shade to cover ribbon ends.

BOLD *black & white*

Recycling success is at its best whenever you can take an overlooked item and make it appealing once again.

Recycled item: a wooden ladder-back chair with woven seat.

You will need: white, black, and yellow acrylic paints; 2" length of $5/8$" dia. plastic tubing; paintbrushes; primer; sealer; and any additional supplies list in Step 1.

1. Read **Surface Preparation** and **Painting A Chair**, page 157.

2. Prepare chair for painting. Paint front legs, bottom leg rungs, and top and bottom chair back rungs black. Paint remaining chair white.

3. For circles on top and bottom chair back rungs, dip one end of plastic tubing in white paint;

touch to surface of chair. Add black stripes to front chair leg rung and middle chair back rungs. Add black and white dots to legs and chair back spindles.

4. Paint seat yellow.

5. Apply sealer to chair.

"THYME" FOR *flowers*

When the cane seat of a chair wears out, don't send it to a landfill. Let it have a second life as a colorful plant stand!

Recycled item: a wooden chair with broken caned seat.

You will need: cream, light purple, and grey-blue acrylic paints; paintbrushes; purple and green permanent medium-point markers; clay flowerpot to fit in hole of seat; primer; sealer; and any additional supplies list in Step 1.

1. Read **Surface Preparation**, **Painting A Chair**, and **Transferring Patterns**, page 157.

2. Prepare chair for painting. Paint chair cream, grey-blue, and light purple, referring to photo for color placement. Paint a $1^3/_4$" x $8^5/_8$" cream rectangle with purple border on top chair back rung.

3. Transfer patterns, page 154, to seat back rungs. Use markers to draw over words and vines.

4. Apply sealer to chair.

5. Thin cream paint with water. Paint flowerpot. Place flowerpot through seat of chair.

This chalkboard tray gets out the word—guests and springtime are always welcome here!

Recycled item: a metal tray with filigree border (ours measures 18½"w x 13½"h x 1¾"d).

You will also need: painter's masking tape, black chalkboard paint, paintbrush, 1½"w purple and gold variegated wire-edged ribbon, hot glue gun, and a silk hydrangea cluster and leaves removed from stem.

Use caution when working with glue gun.

1. Mask off inner sides of tray. Paint inside bottom of tray with chalkboard paint; allow to dry, then remove tape.

2. For hanger, knot ends of a length of ribbon around filigree border. Notch ribbon ends.

3. Hot glue hydrangea cluster and leaves to top edge of tray.

PURSE *planter*

Follow your sense of whimsy to find new cachepots all around you. For instance, a wicker purse blooms into a wonderful planter.

Recycled item: wicker or straw purse and a scrap of ribbon.

You will also need: potted plants with saucer bottoms.

1. Place potted plant in purse.

2. Tie handles of purse together with ribbon.

There's something magical about a wind chime, especially when it's an earth-friendly creation like this.

Recycled item: small wicker basket without handle, broken china pieces, small metal spoons, and wire clothes hangers.

You will also need: spray primer, copper spray paint, spray paint for basket, clear nylon line, pliers, wire cutters, and glue.

1. Spray paint basket.

2. Cut wire hangers into six 10" lengths. Spray with primer, then copper spray paint.

3. For hanger, use pliers to make a curve at the end of one wire length. Insert curved end of wire through bottom of basket; bend wire end into a loop to secure. Bend and curve wire. Make a loop in other end of wire; thread nylon line through loop and knot ends together.

4. Wrap wire around china pieces; use pliers to make a loop at the end of wire for hanger.

5. Hang spoons and china pieces from basket rim using nylon line. Place a small dot of glue on each knot to secure.

WINDOW *message board*

The window frame organizer, with cork area and chalkboard, will make sure you stay too busy to daydream out the window.

Recycled item: a wood-frame window with three panes (we found ours at a flea market).

You will need: sandpaper, tack cloth, ivory and gold acrylic paint, crackling medium, paintbruses, hardboard, saw, sheet cork, white cardstock, spray adhesive, fabric, hot glue gun, chalkboard paint, and glazier's points.

1. Remove and discard glass from window. Scrape away any caulk or sealer; sand window frame and wipe with tack cloth.

2. Using gold paint for base coat and ivory for top coat, follow crackle medium manufacturer's instructions to paint window.

3. For each pane, measure opening; cut a piece of hardboard ¼" larger on all sides than opening.

4. For message board, cut a sheet of cork the same size as one hardboard piece. Use spray adhesive to attach cork to smooth side of hardboard.

5. Cut fabric 1" larger on all sides than one hardboard piece. Center hardboard on wrong side of fabric; pulling fabric taut and folding at corners, wrap fabric edges to wrong side and use hot glue to secure.

6. Scan and print images, pages 155 - 156, onto cardstock. Trim copy to appropriate size; use spray adhesive to attach to center of fabric-covered board.

7. Follow manufacturer's instructions to apply chalkboard paint to smooth side of remaining piece of hardboard.

8. Use glazier's points to mount each hardboard piece in one window opening.

PROJECT *patterns*

valentine suncatchers
(page 12)

artfully alfresco table
(page 23)

valentine suncatchers
(page 12)

jazzy snowman
(page 26)

bird bungalows
(page 8)

paper album
(page 37)

144

cutting line

folding line

itty-bitty gift boxes
(page 48)

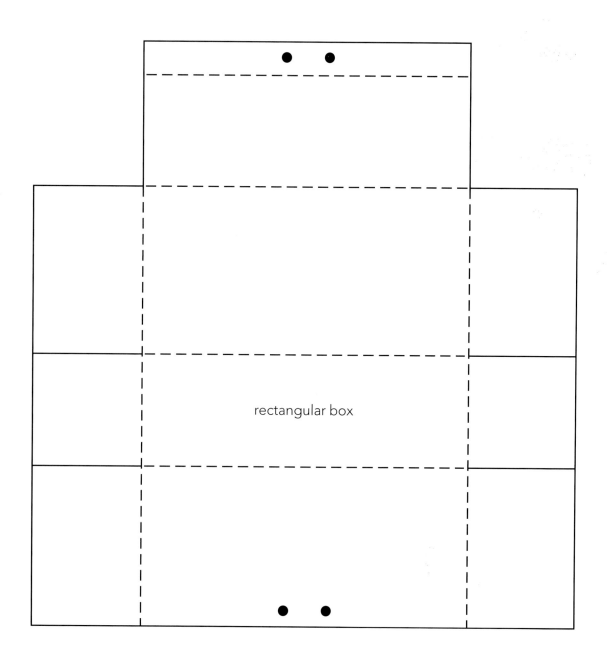

rectangular box

itty-bitty gift boxes
(page 48)

cutting line

folding line

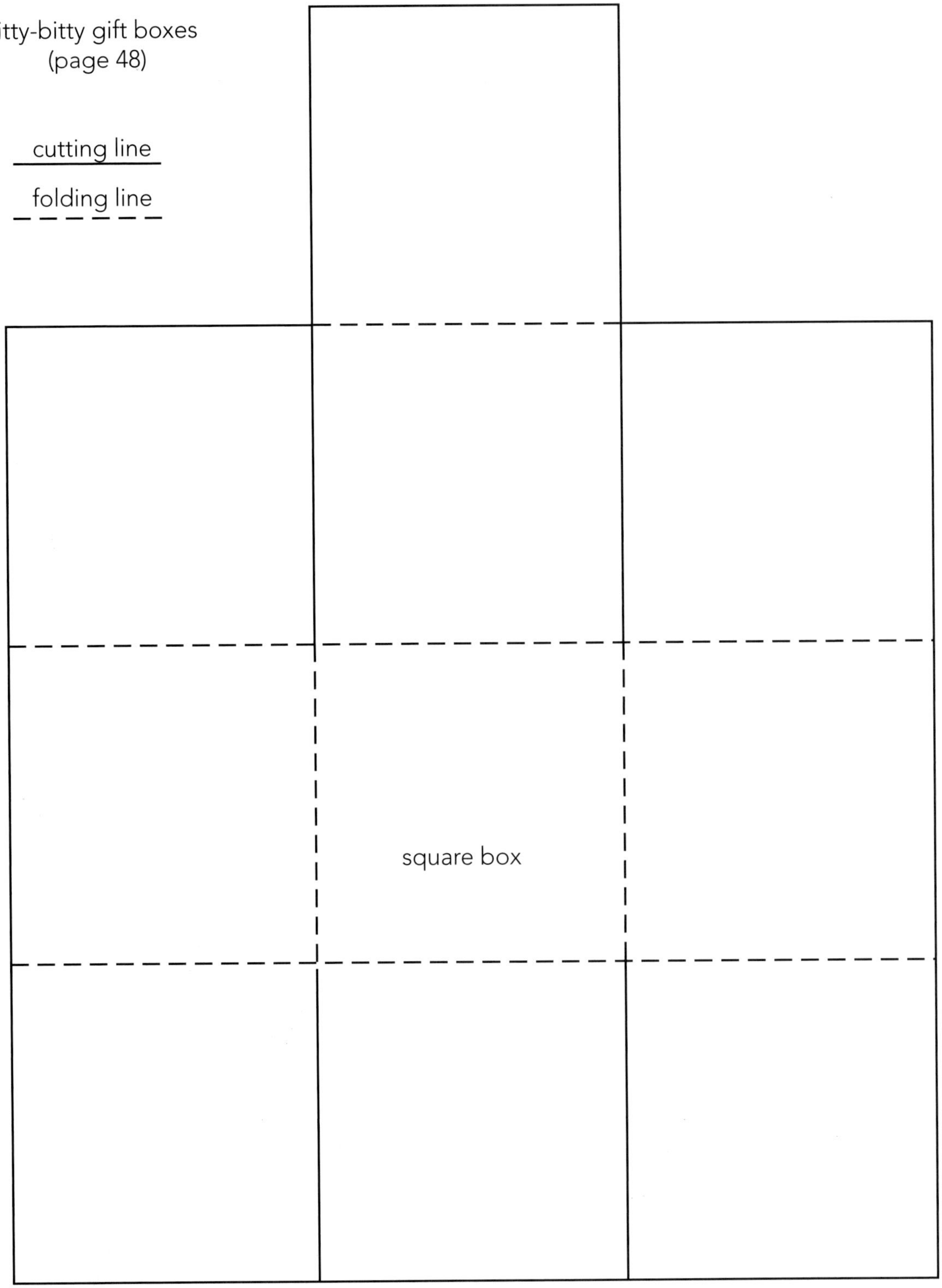

square box

valentine vases
(page 56)

garden greenery lamp
(page 70)

147

floral delight lamp
(page 68)

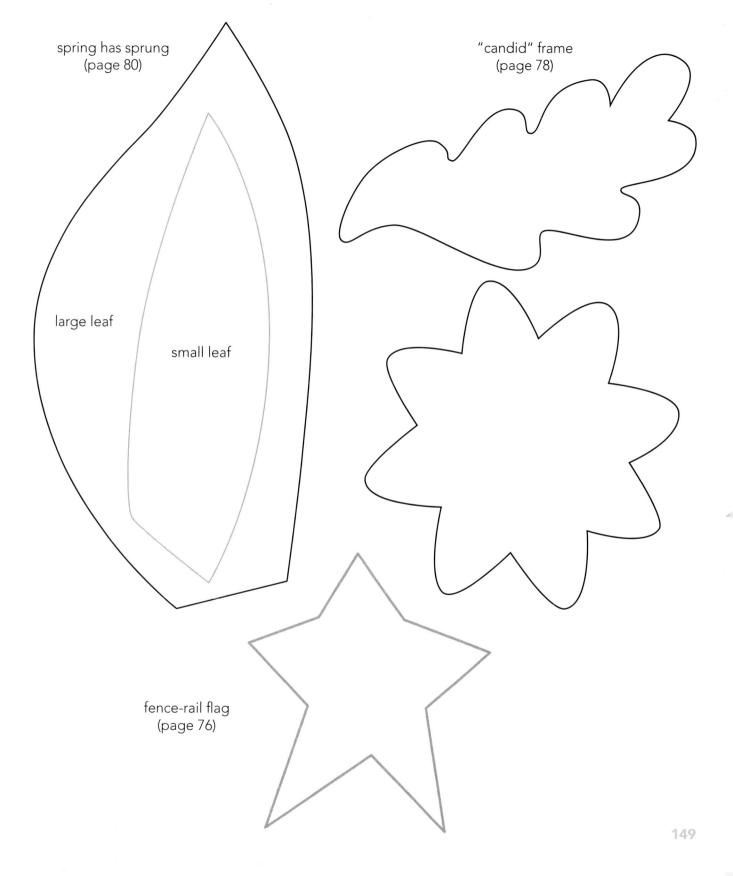

spring has sprung
(page 80)

"candid" frame
(page 78)

large leaf

small leaf

fence-rail flag
(page 76)

creative halloween cans
(page 88)

wiggle worm
(page 111)

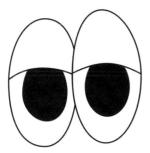

jazzy jean letters
(page 112)

151

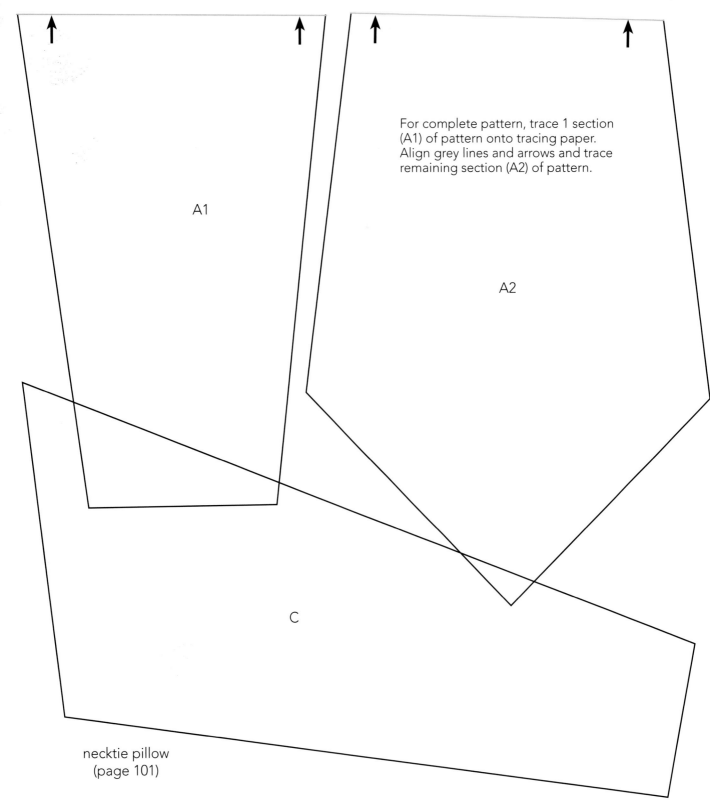

A1

A2

For complete pattern, trace 1 section
(A1) of pattern onto tracing paper.
Align grey lines and arrows and trace
remaining section (A2) of pattern.

C

necktie pillow
(page 101)

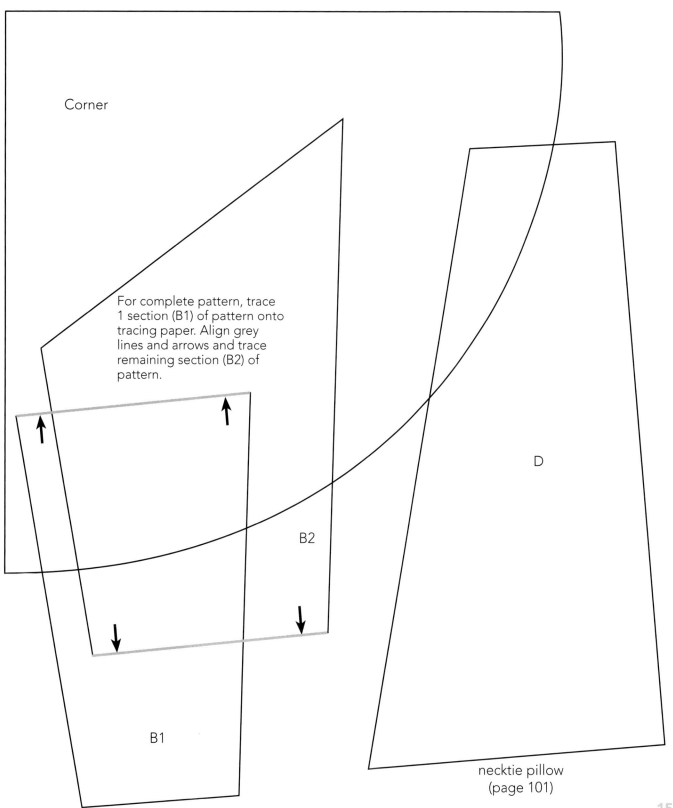

Corner

For complete pattern, trace
1 section (B1) of pattern onto
tracing paper. Align grey
lines and arrows and trace
remaining section (B2) of
pattern.

B2

B1

D

necktie pillow
(page 101)

Take Thyme · To Smell · · The Flowers ·

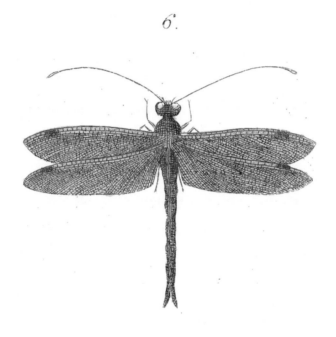

6.

5.

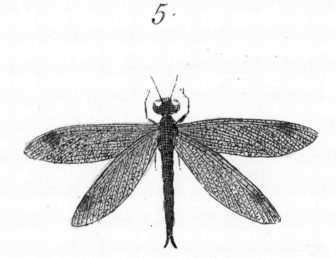

GENERAL *instructions*

PAINTING

SURFACE PREPARATION

Caution: Work in a well-ventilated area when using cleaners. Wear protective gloves and clothing as needed. Cover work area with plastic or newspaper.

You will need: household cleaner, sponge or scouring pad, a soft damp cloth. You may also need: fine grit sandpaper or steel wool, tack cloth, painter's masking tape, and spray primer.

1. Remove any hardware from item.

2. Use cleaner and either sponge or scouring pad to clean item. Remove cleaner with damp cloth; allow to dry. If necessary, repair any holes, cracks, or other imperfections and sand item smooth. Wipe clean with tack cloth; allow to dry.

3. (*Note:* Use masking tape to mask off glass or other items not to be finished.) Follow project instructions to apply finishes.

4. Replace hardware.

PAINTING A CHAIR

You will need: painter's masking tape, kraft paper, primer, paint, and paintbrushes.

1. Mask off any area you don't wish to paint. Use masking tape and kraft paper as needed.

2. Apply primer to prepared surface before painting. Paint will go on more smoothly and it will adhere to surface better.

3. In most cases, you will need to paint the entire chair a single background color before you transfer the patterns and add decorative details. Apply paint using a paintbrush designed for the type of paint you are using, or you may use spray paint. Both types of paint may require more than one coat for even coverage.

Once the background color is dry, follow individual project instructions to transfer patterns, if any, and to paint details.

TRANSFERRING PATTERNS

You will need: tracing paper, transfer paper, and a dull pencil.

Trace pattern onto tracing paper.

Position tracing paper on surface; slide transfer paper between tracing paper and surface. Use a dull pencil to trace over all lines of the pattern.

PAINTING TECHNIQUES

Place project on a covered work surface. To achieve the desired results, practice painting techniques before beginning project. A foam plate makes a good palette.

Painting Basecoats

Select a paintbrush according to project size; for example, when painting a large item, use a large flat brush; when painting a small item, select a small brush. Several coats may be necessary for even coverage. Allow paint to dry after each coat.

Painting Dots

Dip the tip of a round paintbrush, the handle end of a paintbrush, the new eraser on a pencil, or one end of a toothpick in paint and touch to project; dip in paint each time for uniform dots.

Spatter Painting

To spatter paint, dip bristle tips of toothbrush in paint and pull thumb across bristles over project. Repeat as desired.

Sponge Painting

Paint project with basecoat and allow to dry before moving to next color.

To sponge paint surface, use a pouncing or stamping motion, changing the direction of the sponge every few presses and slightly overlapping areas. Reapplying paint to sponge as necessary, fill any missing areas, but still allow the basecoat color to show through. Rinse sponge before using next color.

Painting With Dimensional Paint

Turn bottle upside down to fill tip before each use. While painting, clean up often with a paper towel. If tip becomes clogged, insert a straight pin into opening to unclog.

To paint, touch tip to project. Squeezing and moving bottle steadily, apply paint to project, being careful not to flatten paint line. If painting detail lines, center line of paint over transferred line on project or freehand details as desired.

To correct mistake, use a paring knife to gently scrape excess paint from project before it dries. Carefully remove stain with non-acetone nail polish remover on a cotton swab. A mistake may also be camouflaged by incorporating it into the design.

DÉCOUPAGE

1. Cut motifs from paper and arrange on item to determine desired placement. Remove motifs.

2. Use foam brush to apply a thin layer of glue to 1 area of item to be decoupaged. Brush glue lightly until it becomes tacky. Apply motifs to glued area; use fingertips or cloth to smooth out bubbles and wrinkles, working from centers of motifs outward. (**Note:** Some wrinkles will disappear as glue dries.) Use a damp cloth to gently remove excess glue. If motifs overlap, apply glue over placed motif, then place next motif on item. Repeat to apply remaining motifs. After applying all motifs, allow item to dry.

3. Apply two to three coats of clear acrylic spray sealer to project, allowing to dry after each application.

WORKING WITH WAX

Caution: Do not melt wax over an open flame or in a pan placed directly on burner.

1. Cover work area with newspaper.

2. Heat 1" of water in a saucepan to boiling. Add water as necessary.

3. Place wax and old candles in a large can. If pouring wax, pinch top rim of can to form a spout.

4. To melt wax and candles, place can in boiling water and reduce heat to simmer. Use a craft stick to stir, if necessary.

COVERING OUTSIDE OF BOX

1. Cut a piece of fabric large enough to cover box. Center box on wrong side of fabric and draw around box.

2. Use ruler to draw lines 1/2" outside drawn lines, extending lines to edges of fabric. Draw diagonal lines from intersections of outer lines to corners of original lines.

3. Cut away corners of fabric and clip along diagonal lines (Fig. 1).

Fig. 1

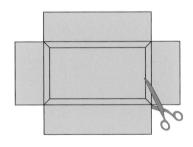

4. Apply spray adhesive to wrong side of fabric.

5. Center box on fabric, matching box to original drawn lines; smooth fabric on bottom of box.